THE
CITIZEN
JOURNALIST'S
PHOTOGRAPHY HANDBOOK

CARLOS MILLER

THE CITIZEN JOURNALIST'S

PHOTOGRAPHY HANDBOOK

ILEX

SHOOTING THE WORLD AS IT HAPPENS

CON T

First published in the UK in 2014 by:

ILEX
210 High Street
Lewes, East Sussex BN7 2NS
www.ilex-press.com

Distributed worldwide (except North America)
by Thames & Hudson Ltd., 181A High Holborn,
London WC1V 7QX, United Kingdom

Copyright © 2014 The Ilex Press Limited

Publisher: Alastair Campbell
Associate Publisher: Adam Juniper
Managing Editors: Natalia Price-Cabrera & Nick Jones
Specialist Editor: Frank Gallaugher
Editorial Assistant: Rachel Silverlight
Creative Director: James Hollywell
Art Director: Julie Weir
Design: Kate Haynes
Colour Origination: Ivy Press Reprographics

British Library Cataloguing-in-Publication Data
A catalogue record for this book is available
from the British Library.

All images are credited to their respective copyright
owners, as indicated in the Picture Credits on page 159.

ISBN: 978-1-78157-984-8

Printed and bound in China

10 9 8 7 6 5 4 3 2 1

THE RISE OF CITIZEN JOURNALISM

OCCUPY WALL STREET, NEW YORK, 2011

FOR THE FIRST TIME IN HISTORY, WE, THE PEOPLE, HAVE TRUE FREEDOM OF THE PRESS WHERE IT IS NO LONGER RESTRICTED TO THOSE WHO OWN THE PRESS. AND THAT IS REVOLUTIONARY CONSIDERING ALL WE NEED IS A SMARTPHONE, AN INTERNET CONNECTION, AND A DESIRE TO SHARE NEWS WITH THE WORLD TO MAKE AN IMPACT.

It could be a mundane photo from a local town hall meeting posted on Facebook, informing citizens of a controversial ordinance being passed. Or a shocking video of police abuse posted on YouTube, taking the internet by storm and earning you thousands of viewers, as well as a few extra dollars in your pocket. Or on-the-spot reports posted on Twitter or Instagram of mass demonstrations in city streets, providing uncensored views of political unrest as it unravels throughout the world.

This democratization of journalism that enables every man, woman and child to report the news, regardless of professional, educational, cultural or economic background is called "citizen journalism"—a phenomenon that has spread in popularity throughout the world over the past decade with the emergence of social media platforms and the increasing affordability and portability of digital cameras.

I prefer to call it "independent journalism" because citizen journalism is usually associated with amateur journalism. And by the time you finish this book, you will not only know how to get paid for your work, you will have more skills than many mainstream media reporters, especially with regards to obtaining public records and how to market yourself as an independent journalist. However, I will mostly use the term citizen journalism in this book because it is the term most commonly used since the turn of the century.

Many times, citizen journalism is accidental, a result of being at the right place at the right time. An example is Jānis Krūms' picture of a US Airways plane that had plunged into the Hudson River in New York City on January 15, 2009. This image was retweeted thousands of times and it was printed on the cover of many newpapers. Other times, citizen journalism is more deliberate and organized, with citizens building online communities that rival the audiences of many traditional newspapers. This new form of journalism has given a powerful voice to the masses who up until recently were restricted to being the silent audiences for traditional media.In that regard, citizen journalism is also a form of activism, a refusal to stay silent in a world of constant upheaval.

And it couldn't have come at a better time considering a handful of media companies control the majority of mainstream news companies after two decades of continuing corporate consolidation. But with that power necessarily comes responsibility and respect for the craft of journalism as well as an understanding of media laws and ethics, which is what you will learn in this book.

I spent almost a decade writing and taking photos for daily newspapers before launching my blog, *Photography is Not a Crime*, which started as a scrappy one-man blog covering a trial in Miami before it morphed into a multi-writer news site covering First Amendment abuses throughout the United States; a site read by lawyers, journalists, students, retirees, activists, photographers, judges, and police officers. I will show you that there is rarely a greater freedom than being able to self publish.

NATIONAL ELECTION, PARIS, 2013

HISTORY OF CITIZEN JOURNALISM

(from JFK to Rodney King)

8MM BELL & HOWELL ZOOMATIC DIRECTOR SERIES MODEL 414PD

NEVER HAVING WORKED AS A JOURNALIST BEFORE, ABRAHAM ZAPRUDER STOOD ON A CONCRETE PILLAR HOLDING HIS HOME MOVIE CAMERA AS PRESIDENT JOHN F. KENNEDY'S MOTORCADE CAME INTO VIEW. IT WAS 1963 AND THE 58-YEAR-OLD CLOTHES MANUFACTURER STEADIED HIS VIEWFINDER AS HIS RECEPTIONIST HELD HIS LEGS FROM BELOW TO KEEP HIM FROM LOSING HIS BALANCE.

When the president's convertible limo came into view, Zapruder, a Russian immigrant and loyal democrat, panned the camera on Kennedy and his wife in the back seat, capturing the motorcade winding south on Elm Street. Zapruder heard a loud bang but thought it was just a car exhaust pipe backfiring. He filmed Kennedy hunching over and grabbing his neck, but figured the president was just playing to the crowd, merely acting as if he had just been shot. When the second shot rang out (really the third, but he didn't hear the first), Zapruder filmed the president's head exploding. In the ensuing chaos as the First Lady tried to crawl out of the presidential limo, bystanders ran for cover, and several professional photojournalists were too stunned to lift their cameras. Zapruder followed the scene with his camera, capturing what would be the most significant piece of evidence in the Kennedy assassination.

It would also go down as the very first citizen journalism video to go viral. Immediately after the shooting, Zapruder gave a copy of his film to the U.S. Secret Service, then sold full rights to the film to *Life* magazine, who paid him $150,000, which would be around a million dollars in today's currency. *Life* magazine published 31 black-and-white photos in its weekly issue, then nine color photos in a special memorial issue two weeks later. The Zapruder film has since been featured in various movies, including Oliver Stone's *JFK* and *In the Line of Fire* starring Clint Eastwood; it can be found on a multitude of YouTube accounts. The 26-second clip was captured on an 8mm Bell & Howell Zoomatic Director Series Model 414PD, a top-of-the-line model at the time, even though it was unable to record audio. Zapruder had purchased the camera a year earlier for more than $200 (more than $1,500 today) and had planned to use it to film his grandchildren. He never picked up another camera for the rest of his life.

Then there is George Holliday, a plumber by trade, who was awakened one night in 1991 by the sounds of police sirens and helicopters outside his Los Angeles apartment. He grabbed his brand new Sony Handycam analog camcorder, which was still in the box, and began recording several LAPD officers beating a young black man relentlessly in what became known as the Rodney King video. Holliday dropped the video off to a local news station who paid him a measly $500.

The video ended up being aired on news stations throughout the country, which led to the trial of four police officers, and major riots in Los Angeles when they were acquitted. The Rodney King video is considered to be the birth of modern-day citizen journalism, especially with regards to documenting police abuse, but at that point, it was still dependent on "old media." But that all changed at the turn of the century when a group of anti-capitalistic activists bypassed the media altogether by launching their own news site called the Independent Media Center.

RODNEY KING BEATING, LOS ANGELES, 1991

Indymedia, as it is commonly called, was launched in November 1999 to report on the activism surrounding the World Trade Organization Ministerial Conference in Seattle, giving readers a different perspective than what was being reported by the mainstream media. Today, Indymedia has websites based in cities throughout the world.

But it wasn't until after the September 11, 2001 terrorist attacks that the general public discovered the power of citizen journalism. Smartphones had yet to be introduced, so only a tiny percentage of citizens were carrying cameras at any given moment, mostly as hobbyists, tourists, students or professionals. One of them was Carmen Taylor, a tourist visiting New York City from Arkansas, who was sitting on a ferry with her Sony Mavica photographing the skyline as the second plane struck the second tower. She snapped two photos; one of the plane about to strike the tower, the second of the tower exploding. After stepping off the ferry, she showed her images to bewildered officer workers who were trying to figure out what had just taken place when a man suggested she use his email at his office to send the photos to a local television station. The Associated Press ended up buying the photo rights, where they ran in numerous publications throughout the world the following day. Over the next few days as the dust settled, witnesses and survivors began posting personal stories and photos on the internet,

GAY RIGHTS RALLY, MIAMI, 2008

WISCONSIN STATE CAPTIAL PROTEST, 2011

mostly through existing blogs or blogs they had created in the wake of the attacks, further planting the seeds of citizen journalism.

Citizen journalism continued to emerge over the next few years with the introduction of cell phone cameras along with the introduction of Facebook, YouTube and Twitter. Not since the invention of the Gutenberg Press in the 15th century had there been such a significant impact on the world of mass communications. At first, most professional journalists ignored this phenomenon, writing it off as a bunch of amateurs producing subpar content. But the media couldn't ignore the impact citizen journalism made with the videos from the 2009 New Year's Day police shooting of Oscar Grant (pages 150–153) or the 2010 Arab Spring uprisings in the Middle East (pages 130–133) or the 2011 Occupy Wall Street protests (pages 146–149). Today, there is little doubt that citizen journalism can be just as powerful, influential, and credible as the largest media company in the world, if not more so.

WORLD TRADE CENTER, MANHATTAN, SEPTEMBER 11, 2001

THE CASE FOR CITIZEN JOURNALISM

1906 CARTOON OF MUCKRAKERS ON THEIR CRUSADE

THROUGHOUT THE 20TH CENTURY, AMERICANS CAME TO TRUST THE MEDIA AS THE FOURTH ESTATE, THE EVER-PRESENT WATCHDOG OVER GOVERNMENT AFFAIRS DOING ITS BEST TO KEEP POLITICIANS HONEST. BUT THE MEDIA TODAY IS FAR TOO INSTITUTIONALIZED TO BE A TRUE VOICE OF THE PEOPLE, SO AMERICANS ARE NOT NEARLY AS TRUSTING OF IT AS THEY USED TO BE.

However, things were much different in the early 1900s with the muckrakers, who exposed corruption and called for big business reform in their newspaper and magazine exposés. And that watchdog style of journalism continued into the 1950s with CBS broadcast journalist Edward R. Murrow going on a crusade against Senator Joe McCarthy, leading to the downfall of the Red Scare perpetrator who had destroyed the careers of thousands of Americans suspected of having communist views.

Media influence was so strong that in 1968, CBS newsman Walter Cronkite, dubbed "the most trusted man in America," was credited for changing public opinion of the Vietnam War when he reported there was no foreseeable way for the United States to emerge as victors, which is believed to have led to President Lyndon B. Johnson dropping out of the race.

And it became even stronger during the early 1970s when *Washington Post* reporters Bob Woodward and Carl Bernstein forced the resignation of President Richard Nixon by exposing the Watergate Scandal, leading to a sharp increase in journalism school applicants throughout the rest of the decade.

With the introduction of cable news in the 1980s and with many cities still having two newspapers (although this had been declining steadily since the introduction of television news), the field was wide open for aspiring journalists who wanted to make a difference.

However, that all started changing in the ensuing years when the Federal Communications Commission began loosening restrictions on media ownership where companies were eventually allowed to buy newspapers, television stations and radio stations within a single market, leading to a drastic reduction in competition among news companies, and a significant reduction in investigative journalism.

In 1980, 50 companies controlled 90% of the American media. By 2013, six companies controlled 90 percent of the media, meaning the muckrakers

of yesteryear would be unable to rail against big business because big business would never publish their articles. Unless, of course, these muckrakers turned to the internet as independent journalists.

The truth is, citizen journalism is a throwback to the pamphleteers of the 18th century who shaped the opinion of American colonists leading up to the Revolutionary War.

Even as newspapers became more established in the 19th century, they remained opinionated, divisive and partisan where before, they were mostly unified in overthrowing the British monarchy and creating a new government.

It wasn't until newspapers began expanding in circulation and in advertising in the latter part of the 19th century that they started becoming objective in order to appeal to as many people as possible, which makes sense from a business perspective. However, today's mass conglomeration of media

THOMAS PAINE, WITH *RIGHTS OF MAN*

companies has created a monolithic monopoly on the industry, resulting in an institutionalized and impersonal style of journalism that has become way too predictable.

Citizen journalists, on the other hand, are providing thought-provoking analysis, hyper-local stories and unfiltered videos of real issues affecting real people.

THE CASE AGAINST

(& why it's wrong)

THE BEST THING ABOUT CITIZEN JOURNALISM IS ITS INDEPENDENCE AND LACK OF HIERARCHICAL MANAGEMENT. BUT THAT COULD ALSO BE ITS WORST ATTRIBUTE, ESPECIALLY IF THERE IS NO TRANSPARENCY INVOLVED. WITH NO EDITORIAL OVERSIGHT OR PROFESSIONAL GUIDELINES, AND AT TIMES NO JOURNALISTIC ETHICS AND INTEGRITY, CITIZEN JOURNALISTS CAN OFTEN BE RECKLESS AND DANGEROUS WITH THEIR REPORTING, EITHER INTENTIONALLY OR UNINTENTIONALLY.

In 2008, an anonymous commenter on CNN's iReport site for citizen journalists reported that Apple CEO Steve Jobs had been rushed to the hospital following a heart attack—a report that turned out to be false. Nevertheless, the rumor spread like a virus throughout the internet, causing Apple's stocks to plummet within an hour. Even after Apple had publicly denied the rumor and CNN had removed the post, the news continued to spread via social media. It caused such a huge drop in stock that the United States Securities and Exchanges Commission launched an investigation to see if the false report was a deliberate attempt to manipulate stock. It turns out that it was just an 18-year-old man who said he was bored and wanted to have some fun.

Then in 2009, a pair of conservative activists named James O'Keefe and Hannah Giles teamed up to produce a series of undercover videos aimed at the Association of Community Organizations for Reform Now

(ACORN), a non-profit organization that conducted voter registration drives in low-income neighborhoods. O'Keefe and Giles posed as a pimp and prostitute as they secretly recorded ACORN workers appearing to advise the couple on how to avoid paying taxes while hiding their illegal activity. The videos were aired on Fox News, causing several employees to lose their jobs as well as millions of dollars to be lost in funding, forcing the organization to file for bankruptcy.

But then investigations by attorney generals in several states determined the videos were heavily edited and had included false and misleading information. An ensuing investigation by the U.S. Government Accountability Office determined ACORN workers had not misused government funds or participated in criminal activity as purported in the videos. O'Keefe and Giles ended up paying $150,000 in a settlement to one of the fired workers whom they had secretly recorded because they had violated California's eavesdropping law.

THE ROCKAWAYS, QUEENS, NEW YORK, 2012

In 2012, as Hurricane Sandy tore through New York City, an unconfirmed report began making the rounds on Twitter that the New York Stock Exchange was flooded with three feet of water. The tweet ended up reported on television by CNN and The Weather Channel, naturally sending out a panic wave with investors throughout the country. The report, of course, turned out to be false, prompting the networks to correct themselves and blame the inaccuracy on the chaos of the storm. The truth is, there is plenty of bad citizen journalism out there, some of it meant to deliberately mislead, most of it just a result of sloppy reporting and editing. By the time you finish this book, you will have the skills, ethics and legal knowledge that will ensure you're not one of the bad ones.

THE ETHICS

WE ARE LIVING IN AN AGE WHEN ANYBODY CAN PUBLISH ANYTHING ON THE INTERNET AND CALL THEMSELVES A JOURNALIST. AND WE'VE SEEN COUNTLESS EXAMPLES OF THESE SO-CALLED JOURNALISTS OVER THE YEARS WHO END UP MISLEADING PEOPLE WITH THEIR STAGED VIDEOS, MANIPULATED PHOTOS OR FABRICATED TWEETS THAT END UP MAKING THE ROUNDS ON SOCIAL MEDIA PLATFORMS FOR DAYS, SOMETIMES WEEKS.

Many times they do it for kicks, but many times they do it to meet their personal agenda. But once it has been revealed that they have deliberately misled people—and it almost always happens—then they lose credibility as truth-tellers. And that's the last thing you want as a citizen journalist. After all, journalism is foremost about reporting the truth. Even if it's the truth as you see it, which may be different than the truth somebody else sees. This is where transparency comes in.

Transparency vs. Objectivity

For more than a century, journalists have been encouraged to remain objective in the stories they report as they present both sides of an issue, allowing the reader to decide. Maintaining a sense of institutionalized neutrality makes sense from a business perspective because it allows news companies to report the news without having to take an actual stance, which could turn off advertisers and governmental sources. But nobody is truly ever objective. We all have our opinions. We all have our biases. And we all see the world through

CARIBBEAN FESTIVAL, MIAMI, 2013

our own experiences. Besides, some cable news networks don't even come close to remaining objective while claiming otherwise. And although most news companies and organizations maintain very straightforward ethical guidelines, it's not difficult to find reporters who break them. That is why transparency is much more credible than objectivity. And this mostly comes in the form of disclosure.

If you have a personal agenda to your reporting, then disclose it. If you are associated with a certain politician, then disclose it. If you are receiving money or freebies from businesses in exchange for promotion, then disclose it (which is actually required by the Federal Trade Commission). And if you make a mistake, which we all do from time to time, own up to it. Otherwise, you're not only ruining your credibility but making it more difficult for other those citizen journalists striving for credibility.

Staged or Manipulated Photos

In 2012, Swedish photojournalist Paul Hansen photographed a group of men carrying the bodies of two Palestinian children through the streets of Gaza, who were killed during an Israeli air attack. The photo, which he named Gaza Burial, ended up winning the 2013 World Press Photo contest for best photo.

But the photo immediately came under scrutiny by critics throughout the world who accused Hansen of combining several frames in order to get that perfect shot, which would be a huge ethics violation and grounds to have his prize revoked. However, an independent forensics examination eventually determined the photo was retouched within the acceptable boundaries of photojournalism and Hansen was allowed to keep his prize.

However, there have been several other professional photojournalists who have been disqualified from contests when it was discovered they had digitally removed objects or people from their photos in order to make for a better composition. Photojournalism is about capturing what you see with the naked eye, not what you wish you would have captured had there not been that annoying distraction. Cropping a photo to remove unnecessary distractions is pretty much always acceptable, as is adjusting basic toning and lighting levels to allow viewers to better evaluate the scene (after all, cameras are not always as competent at capturing images as the human eye). You also want to avoid shooting staged or recreated photos, as tempting as it may be. Or if you do decide to shoot a staged or recreated photo, then be sure to disclose that important detail in the caption. But doing so would be a painstaking reminder that you missed

PALESTINIAN RALLY, MIAMI, 2008

photographing the original incident, so it's best to avoid that altogether.

Undercover Videos

Some of the best (and worst) journalistic work has come to light because of undercover videography. We mentioned

James O'Keefe on page 14 and his undercover work on ACORN. The truth is, he has done a whole series of similar videos against his political opponents. He might believe he is doing the right thing by exposing (or creating) questionable statements for the benefits of his ideology, but he has been written off in the journalistic community as being highly unethical with very little credibility. However, he also has a very strong fan base who believe in everything he does.

There are also many animal rights activists who resort to undercover videos to expose abuse within farms that have led to animal cruelty charges against farm employees. In turn, the farming industry has lobbied for the introduction of laws that prohibit these types of videos. But the National Press Photographers Association (NPPA) was one of 70 organizations to lobby against these so called "ag-gag" bills, which they deemed a crackdown on whistleblowers.

Unlike laws, there is no black and white when it comes to ethics (and many times, laws can be interpreted differently, which is why he have trials). But several journalism organizations have drafted codes of ethics, including the Society of Professional Journalists, the National Press Photographers Association, and the National Public

Radio. There is even a Streamer Journalist Code of Ethics that was drafted for livestreamers (all of which can be found through Google), and they all stress accuracy, fairness and integrity.

CONFRONTATION ON THE BROOKLYN BRIDGE, OWS, 2011

CITIZEN PROFILE: CARLOS MILLER

MY STORY: THE BIRTH OF A BLOG

IN 2007, I WAS ON ASSIGNMENT FOR A LOCAL WEBSITE IN MIAMI WORKING ON A STORY ABOUT A CRIME-RIDDEN NEIGHBORHOOD UNDERGOING POSITIVE CHANGES WITH THE OPENING OF SEVERAL TRENDY RESTAURANTS AND COFFEE SHOPS IN THE AREA.

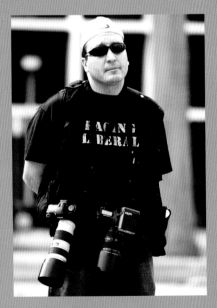

I was walking down Biscayne Blvd, photographing the occasional prostitute and talking to business owners, when I came across a group of police officers on the side of the road, threatening to arrest a man for reasons I did not know. I began taking photos and was quickly ordered away by one of the cops, who informed me that they were dealing with a "private matter." I pointed out that I was in a "public area" and that they had no expectation of privacy. I ended up getting tackled, arrested, and beaten up before spending the night in a jail cell on nine misdemeanor charges, including the false accusation that I had been standing in the middle of the road blocking traffic.

After limping out of jail the following morning, I retrieved my camera from the police station and viewed my photos, discovering that the last series of photos I shot showed the street behind the cops, proving that I had not been blocking traffic as they had claimed. Two days later, I posted my story and photos on *Democratic Underground*, the political forum I used to frequent, and before I knew it, someone had linked it to an aggregating site called *Digg*, where it then ended up on *Boing Boing*, two very popular sites I had never heard of at the time. And from there, the story was picked up by a multitude of blogs in Miami as well as throughout the country, including the popular photography blog run by Thomas Hawk in San Francisco.

My story had not only gone national, an achievement that didn't happen often enough during my newspaper days, it had prompted citizens throughout the country to take a stance on whether or not I deserved getting arrested to the point where they debated for days in the blogosphere and on forums. Meanwhile, with the exception of a few newspaper blurbs and a much-appreciated segment by Local 10's Glenna Milberg, it went ignored in the local media.

Two months after having learned the power of the internet, I launched my blog, *Photography is Not a Crime*, to document my upcoming trial, knowing I couldn't depend on the local media.

Today, my blog receives hundreds of thousands of views a month and has been mentioned in countless mainstream publications, including *Playboy* magazine, *The New York Times* and *The Washington Post*. I have also been invited to speak at a number of national conferences throughout the country to speak about the First Amendment and how it applies to photographers. And I was given the opportunity to write this book. All because I took advantage of the freedom of the press enabled by the internet.

Over the next several chapters, you will read about nine other citizens who also took advantage of this relatively newfound freedom, carving out their own niches by establishing their own brand of independent journalism.

TOOLS OF THE TRADE

DURING THE 1930S AND '40S, A MAN NAMED ARTHUR FELLIG WOULD DRIVE THE STREETS OF NEW YORK CITY PHOTOGRAPHING CRIME SCENES, CELEBRITIES AND ANYTHING NEWSWORTHY THAT HE COULD SELL TO THE PAPERS. NICKNAMED "WEEGEE" AFTER THE OUIJA BOARD GAME FOR HIS KNACK OF BEING AT THE RIGHT PLACE AT THE RIGHT TIME, HE IS CREDITED FOR BEING ONE OF THE ORIGINAL FREELANCE PHOTOJOURNALISTS. BUT IN A SENSE, HE WAS ALSO A CITIZEN JOURNALIST IN THAT HE WAS AN OUTSIDER TO THE ESTABLISHED NEWSPAPER PHOTOGRAPHERS WHO ALL HAD POLICE-ISSUED PRESS CREDENTIALS AND COMPANY-ISSUED CAMERAS.

ARTHUR FELLIG, AKA "WEEGEE" WITH SPEED GRAPHIC, 1944

Weegee had his own gear, including a 4×5 Speed Graphic camera and an automatic flash he never left home without. He also had a police radio, a typewriter, and developing equipment he kept in the trunk of his car, which he used as a darkroom on those occasions he couldn't make it back to his studio apartment in Lower Manhattan. With no formal training, he went on to publish books, consult on Hollywood films and even play a few movie roles. All because he had that knack for being at the right place at the right time, with the right equipment. Things are so much easier today because we don't have to depend on the slow, heavy (but respected) Speed Graphic camera that was the staple of photojournalists for decades. We also don't need to set up darkrooms in the trunks of our cars in order to get our photos published. We can do all that from our smartphone in a fraction of the time it took Weegee. But, then again, so can everybody else.

The key to being a successful citizen journalist is to be like Weegee and set yourself apart from the others. Back in

Weegee's day, New York City boasted dozens of daily newspapers, so he had a large market to which to sell his photos. But he also had a lot of competition—there was always something happening and no shortage of photojournalists. So after two years of working the scene, he not only received his police-issued press card but talked them into allowing him to use a police radio in his car, which none of the others had, allowing him to arrive at crime scenes before the actual cops on many occasions. That, of course, is how he earned his nickname.

Today, we can access police scanners through our smartphones with the right app. And even if we don't want to spend our days plugged into a scanner, we can still keep up with current events and breaking news through Twitter, Facebook or Google+. But if we really want our images or videos to stand above the rest, we need to invest in more than just a smartphone.

DSLRS

DIGITAL SINGLE-LENS REFLEX CAMERAS HAVE BEEN THE STANDARD OF PROFESSIONAL PHOTOJOURNALISTS FOR A LONG TIME, AND FOR GOOD REASON—THEY PROVIDE ACCESS TO A COMPLETE SYSTEM, FROM LENSES TO FLASHES, WITH A WIDE RANGE OF SPECIALIST EQUIPMENT IN BETWEEN; THEY CAN FOCUS QUICKLY (AND USUALLY ACCURATELY); AND, FOR BETTER OR WORSE, THEY LOOK THE PART.

The basic design of a DSLR hasn't changed since the 1950s. Light passes through the lens and onto a mirror that sits in front of the imaging sensor (previously film). From there, most of that light is reflected up through a prism (or an array of more mirrors) and into the photographer's eye, positioned at the viewfinder on the back of the camera. A small portion of the light is also reflected down into a separate autofocus sensor, which itself can communicate with motors in the lens or camera that drive lens elements into a certain position for optimal focus.

That all sounds complicated, but a half-dozen decades of refinement have made it extremely reliable. It's also made it quite cheap, relatively speaking. Because this technology is so evolved and mature, even entry-level DSLRs are robust devices, with a price-to-performance ratio that professionals of just a decade ago would have drooled over. In fact, if you're in the market, it's often in your best interest to look at last year's models—in pretty much every case, they're still top performers, lacking some new gimmick or gadget, but often priced at a huge discount. You'll be in

good company with a DSLR, particularly with any current Nikon or Canon model—not because they're necessarily better by any metric, but simply because they're by far the most common, allowing you to borrow lenses, familiarize yourself with a common set of controls, and so on.

Speaking of lenses, there are certain lenses that are better suited to photojournalism than others. While prime (or fixed-focal-length, non-zoomable) lenses can be cheaper and better in low light, a zoom lens will give you a a better chance at quality compositions in dynamic, high-action scenarios. The professional standard is often a 70–200mm (35mm-equivalent) zoom, but any telephoto lens will help bring the action to the foreground. On the other hand, if you find yourself deep in the midst of the action, a wide-angle lens, like a 24mm-equivalent lens, has the ability to pull the viewer into the scene and amplify the drama. They're harder to compose with, and require getting very close to your subjects, but if that sounds like your style of shooting, the results can be impressive.

DSLR GEAR GUIDE

PROS:
- UNMATCHED SYSTEM OF LENSES, FLASHES, ACCESSORIES, ETC.
- FAST FOCUS, ESPECIALLY WITH MOVING SUBJECTS

CONS:
- BULKY
- CONSPICUOUS

EQUIPMENT CHECKLIST:
- PLENTY OF MEMORY CARDS
- TELEPHOTO ZOOM
- WIDE-ANGLE PRIME
- EXTERNAL FLASH UNIT

COMPACT SYSTEM CAMERAS

COMPACT SYSTEM CAMERAS (CSCS) EMERGED ON THE PHOTO SCENE BACK IN 2008, AND HAVE EVOLVED RAPIDLY EVER SINCE. STRICTLY BUILT FOR DIGITAL, WITH FEW TIES TO LEGACY FILM SYSTEMS, THESE SYSTEMS SEEK TO OFFER EQUIVALENT PERFORMANCE AND IMAGE QUALITY AS DSLRS, BUT IN A MUCH SMALLER AND LIGHTER PACKAGE—BOTH IN THE CAMERA ITSELF AND THE WIDER SYSTEM OF LENSES AND ACCESSORIES.

The reflex mirror described on page 24 was necessary with film, as there was no other way to see through the lens, and the filmstrip had to be kept in the dark until the moment of exposure. Not so with a digital imaging sensor, however, as it can be live and transmitting an image right up to the moment of exposure. That live image (often called Live View) can be fed to the LCD screen on the back of the camera, or to an electronic eye-level viewfinder. And without the need for a complex mirrorbox and pentaprism assembly, the camera can be designed much smaller.

The significance of a smaller camera system in photojournalism is hard to overstate. There's an immediate, tangible benefit to not being weighed down by several pounds of equipment dangling from your neck, particularly when you're on the street, weaving in and out of crowds and trying to position yourself for a good viewpoint. And beyond mere convenience, being able to maintain a smaller, less obtrusive profile allows access to certain situations and scenes that may not otherwise be off limits without being intrusive. It's one thing to hoist up a

OCCUPY LOS ANGELES RALLY, LOS ANGELES, CALIFORNIA, 2011

OWS ANNIVERSARY ACTION, WINNIPEG, CANADA, 2012

half-meter-long lens to your face and point it straight at your subject, and quite another to angle a lens half that long and use an adjustable LCD screen to frame your shot without ever raising the camera to your face at all. The former invites attention—both from the particants in the action and, possibly, from nearby police; whereas the latter is much more likely to pass unnoticed.

Indeed, along those lines it's worth highlighting the fact that, as unfair as it is, larger DSLR equipment can be immediately suspect in the eyes of nearby authorities—you look less like an innocent bystander and may well be more likely to invite attention by police. Not fair, but that's the reailty. CSCs can let you drift under the radar, allowing you to capture equal-quality shots while maintaining a discreet profile.

As for the lenses, while what I said on page 25 about zoom lenses is true, if you're going for a light and portable system, a prime lens is almost always going to be vastly smaller—you just have to "zoom with your feet" and get where you need to be for the shot.

CSC GEAR GUIDE

PROS:
- VERY INCONSPICUOUS
- HIGHLY MOBILE
- CHEAP (IF YOU LOOK AT LAST YEAR'S MODELS)

CONS:
- SLIGHTLY LESS CAPABLE IN LOW LIGHT
- FOCUS IS OFTEN POOR ON MOVING SUBJECTS

EQUIPMENT CHECKLIST:
- SMALL PRIME LENSES
- LIGHTWEIGHT NECK OR WRISTSTRAP

VIDEO CAMERAS

VIDEO HAS SURGED FORTH AS A MEDIUM THAT PHOTOGRAPHERS AND PHOTOJOURNALISTS ALIKE ARE NOW EXPECTED TO EMBRACE. ITS INCLUSION AS A FEATURE ON VIRTUALLY EVERY CURRENT DIGITAL CAMERA AND SMARTPHONE, COMBINED WITH FAST 3G AND BROADBAND NETWORKS, MAKES IT MORE ACCESSIBLE THAN EVERY BEFORE. NEVERTHELESS, IT'S A DIFFERENT BEAST THAN STILL PHOTOGRAPHY, AND REQUIRES SOME SPECIALIZED SKILLS.

First, it's important to recognize the difference in video capabilities between dedicated video camcorders and digital cameras (CSCs and DSLRs, namely) that include HD video shooting as a feature. The larger sensors contained in the latter set are fantastic for shooting in low light, but focus also becomes much more of a chore due to the much shallower depth of field (the range of acceptably sharp focus in front of and behind your exact plane of focus). If you have the time to set up your lights and position, say, an interview subject at a static distance from the camera, then

it's the perfect tool for the job. However, in more dynamic, on-the-scene situations, the last thing you want to worry about is setting your focus as your subjects move erratically in front of the camera. In such a case, even an inexpensive camcorder may well be the better choice. These have much smaller sensors, which result in a depth of field that can stretch from a few feet in front of the camera all the way to the horizon, without the need for constant refocusing. This kind of cinematography is, in fact, part of the documentary aesthetic. In creative drama, the ability to isolate a thin plane

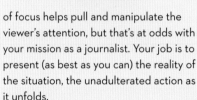

RED-SHIRT PROTEST IN BANGKOK, THAILAND, 2013

of focus helps pull and manipulate the viewer's attention, but that's at odds with your mission as a journalist. Your job is to present (as best as you can) the reality of the situation, the unadulterated action as it unfolds.

It's also important to remember that the audio is often just as important as the video quality. There are numerous examples throughout this book of interactions and scenes where the audio recording was the key piece of the story or evidence—indeed, viewers are quite forgiving of haphazard video quality if there's a clear line of audio. If you find yourself shooting a lot of video, it's absolutely worthwhile to invest in a dedicated accessory microphone, as even camcorders often have mediocre built-in microphones at best. A windguard (it looks like a fuzzy hat that fits over the microphone) can further increase quality by cutting down on ambient noise that may otherwise obscure the clarity of the audio track. Also, during editing, if the audio is still unclear, it's often a good idea to transcribe the audio and overlay subtitles so that nothing gets lost.

VIDEO GEAR GUIDE

PROS:
- EASY TO OPERATE WITH JUST ONE HAND
- TOP-QUALITY VIDEO FILES

CONS:
- REQUIRES POST-PRODUCTION AND EDITING TO OPTIMIZE CONTENT

EQUIPMENT CHECKLIST:
- DEDICATED MICROPHONE WITH WINDGUARD
- PLENTY OF MEMORY CARDS
- TRIPOD (FOR STATIC SHOTS)
- LED PANEL FOR LOW LIGHT

SMARTPHONES

IF THERE'S AN ICON OF CITIZEN JOURNALISM, IT'S THE SMARTPHONE. THEIR SHEER UBIQUITY MEANS THEY'RE OFTEN THE FIRST CAMERA ON THE SCENE OF NEWSWORTHY EVENT, AND THEIR CONNECTIVITY RUNS CIRCLES AROUND EVEN PROFESSIONAL-QUALITY CAMERA SYSTEMS.

I recognize that the term "smartphone" has become extremely generic, with vast differences in the technology inside the various models currently on the market (and I'll stay well away from the operating system debate, as well). But while one may have a better zoom range, or another may have expandable memory, the fundamental principle related to citizen journalism remain the same: It's a mobile publishing platform. You can take photos, shoot video, write brief tweets or long-form articles, and instantly broadcast this media to a variety of sources on the internet.

So, with that said, the most important thing is to make sure you are utilizing your smartphone to its fullest potential. If the action develops rapidly and your smartphone is your only tool, your workflow is pretty straightforward. First, you'll need to get close to the scene, as these cameras are (with rare exceptions) equipped with fixed-focal-length wide-angle lenses. You'll also need to anticipate the action, as there's often quite a bit of lag time between when you press the shutter button and with the image is captured—so press it just before the action reaches its peak.

RED-SHIRT PROTEST IN BANGKOK, THAILAND, 2013

With the photo or video captured, I'd caution against putting a gimmicky filter effect on any newsworthy shots, but cropping is fair game, especially if the important subject takes up only a small portion of the frame.

The next step is distribution. As to where you should upload it to, you have quite a few options. A tweet has become the classic first stop for newsworthy shots. Short and sweet, you simply write up a quick 140-character description of the scene, incorporating clear and straightforward hashtags (the goal being to make the media easily searchable once the news becomes more widespread), and click upload. Other distribution options include dedicated news sites like CNN iReport, Indymedia, and Wikinews, which basically have a perpetual call for any and all newsworthy photos, which can then be cultivated and promoted at an editor's discretion. Such options also give you the chance to flesh out the backstory a fair amount. Of course, if you already run a blog or popular social media account, naturally that will be your first port of call.

I also want to point out how a smartphone can augment your existing workflow with your other dedicated cameras. Wifi and NFC (Near Field Communication) are two technologies that are gradually working their way into newer camera models, allowing you to wirelessly transfer photos off of your camera and onto your phone (and even if your camera lacks this feature, you can still gain the ability by using a WiFi-equipped SD card like the EyeFi). This setup gets you the best of both worlds—professional image quality that can be shared and distributed with ease. Just be sure to shoot JPEG!

Finally, smartphones also come in handy when you find yourself in a police confrontation. By using them to record video the encounter, you'll have a valuable record of exactly what happened in case it even comes down to a court appearance. I strongly recommend using a live-streaming service (like Livestream) or setting up an instant-backup (like DropBox offers) so this record can't be deleted or lost with the destruction of the phone itself.

ESSENTIAL ACCESSORIES

WHILE IT'S IMPORTANT NOT TO WEIGH YOURSELF DOWN WITH TOO MUCH GEAR BEFORE GOING OUT IN THE FIELD, THERE ARE SOME ESSENTIAL ACCESSORIES THAT WILL IMPROVE THE QUALITY OF YOUR SHOTS (BE THEY VIDEO OR STILL), AND EXPEDITE YOUR POST-PRODUCTION WORKFLOW CONSIDERABLY.

Backup cameras: It's only a matter of time before your camera breaks; it's just a fact. If you find yourself diving into protests or other street action, you're likely going to be pushing your gear to its extremes already. So it's imperative to have some sort of backup. I wouldn't recommend going the professional route of having total redundancy and thus carrying around twice as much gear as you need. Instead, look on the market for a cheap point and shoot (they're almost all cheap these days) that you can tuck in a pocket and forget about—until you need it.

Computers/Tablets: If you're going on location—particularly to another state or country—you'll need to edit on the fly if you plan on getting the scoop. You're likely to come back with too many shots to put into a single story, so you need time to evaluate the totality of the shoot on a screen larger than your camera's LCD, and pare down your selects to a refined album that hits all the main points. It's a valuable step that will make the quality of your shots stand out above someone who plasters a facebook wall with hundreds of shots of a protest, half of which aren't even keepers.

Fortunately, if you're shooting JPEG (or at least RAW + JPEG), this really doesn't take much time, and doesn't require a powerful machine at all—indeed, a tablet will work fine, and is much more travel friendly. Even basic video editing can be done on a decent tablet—the newer the better as these will have more powerful processors that can crunch the data much faster. But the more you find yourself delving into Photoshop or Final Cut Pro, the more you should consider using a proper laptop. A top-specced small laptop can easily outperform a run-of-the-mill larger one these days.

Supports: Nobody wants to run around a protest with a tripod, but there are a number of situations that nevertheless benefit from a stable shooting platform. Video is an obvious one, and as I mentioned earlier, if you're shooting a static interview or establishing shot, they're essential. For more chaotic environments, I'd recommend something like the Joby Gorillapod, pictured above. It's small and lightweight, and can clamp its legs around pretty much any surface you can think of. If you need it, you take it out, set it up, get the shot, and throw it back in your bag—easy.

Storage: Your images aren't backed up until they're safely off your volatile memory cards and stored on two separate hard drives—and ideally, one of those hard drives is kept off-site. Cloud storage is an evolving option for the off-site option, but it's such a rapidly changing landscape it's impossible to make a solid recommendation there yet. As for the hard drive: just don't cheap out. These things are so inexpensive already, and your images are so valuable, it's absolutely worth getting a high-quality, rugged drive like the LaCie Rugged Thunderbolt pictured above.

HONOR YOUR OATH

AS A TRUCK DRIVER IN NORTH FLORIDA, JEFF GRAY WOULD FREQUENTLY DRIVE THROUGH SOME OF THE MOST NOTORIOUS SPEED TRAPS IN THE COUNTRY.

These include towns like like Waldo, Hampton and Lawtey, with a total population of maybe two thousand, and about 70 miles from the nearest beach. Nothing more than a pit stop in this tourist-laden state. The towns have been exploiting speed traps for decades, snarling drivers barrelling down U.S. Route 301 where speed limits drop from 65 mph to 55 mph to 45 mph—all the way down to 20 mph during school zone hours—within less than a mile. In fact, the American Automobile Association has long condemned the towns, stating that they use "unfair, unethical or illegal law enforcement tactics" in order to meet their annual budgets, issuing ten times the number of tickets as other towns of similar size.

"I've driven through them over the years and seen them pulling people over and bringing dogs up on their vehicles with their stuff strewn all over the road," he

said. "I knew they were not doing it for safety reasons. They were doing it for revenue reasons."

So in November 2010, at the age of 40, Gray decided to start videotaping the speed traps with the intention of posting the videos online to educate

others planning on driving through the towns. Using an old Canon camcorder that had only been used to tape family gatherings, the married father of three who lives in St. Augustine headed out to Lawley. He pulled into town, careful not to surpass the speed limit, parked his car and stepped out to start videotaping the cops. It wasn't long before he found himself surrounded by several cops, one of them demanding his identification and camera. Even though he knew he was under no legal obligation to hand over either, he obliged, informing them that he was doing so "under duress." They ended up returning his items 20 minutes later, allowing him to be on his way, thinking that they had intimidated him enough where he would never try that again.

They were wrong because it left Gray even more determined to expose their speed traps and to record police in public. Realizing it would be too costly and complicated to convert analog videos to digital to upload online, he purchased a refurbished Panasonic digital camcorder off eBay for $98. He then returned to Lawtey and started pointing out on camera the places where police hide before pulling people over.

In January 2011, he launched his YouTube channel, naming it HONORYOUROATH, fully determined to make cops honor the oath they took upon receiving the badge. He started

CITIZEN PROFILE: JEFF GRAY

posting videos of the speed traps but also started video recording cops any chance he got, including one memorable video from May 2011 where a Florida Highway Patrol officer told him he was not allowed to take pictures of a huge command center vehicle at a gas station. Despite several threats that they would confiscate his camera, Gray continued recording the vehicle, asserting his First Amendment right to record, informing them that they would be violating his Fourth Amendment rights if they confiscated his camera.

"I was very confident that day," he said. "I wasn't scared or nervous at all. I understood that these troopers were making complete fools of themselves and I was capturing their foolishness."

The troopers finally relented, acknowledging that he did have the right to record them and the ensuing video went viral. And he continued posting videos of interactions with police throughout Northern Florida, always making it a point to be cordial and professional, but never succumbing to their attempts of intimidation.

However, in May 2012, he returned to Lawtey and was arrested by a pair of police officers who greeted him by name, knowing exactly who he was, then claiming they didn't know who he was, which is why they needed his identification. They also told him it was illegal to record them without their consent. The charges were quickly dropped as both assertions were false. Citizens are only required to identify themselves to police if there is a reasonable suspicion they have committed a crime. Not to mention nobody, including police, have an expectation of privacy in public, so consent to record is not needed. The arrest made Gray even more determined to continue recording the police.

"I want to remind LEOs (law enforcement officers) that it is their duty to uphold and defend the constitution, not to blindly follow orders and enforce unjust laws," he said.

But not all cops he encounters attempt to violate his constitutional rights. He has had several positive encounters as well, including one memorable video where a Green Cove Springs police officer named Austin Graham gives him a thorough explanation of his radar gun, allowing Gray to video record it up close, a perfect, but rare, example of the police transparency. In fact, that video became his most popular, accumulating more than 200,000 views in two years. Since then, he has expanded his journalistic endeavors into learning and educating others about Florida's extensive public records laws to further hold public officials accountable.

The most important lesson he has learned over the years?

"Back-up cameras. Never go out without back-up cameras."

THE SOCIAL MEDIA EDGE

ON JULY 29, 2010, I ATTEMPTED TO WALK INTO A MIAMI-DADE METRORAIL STATION WITH AN HDNET NEWS CREW THAT HAD FLOWN INTO TOWN TO INTERVIEW ME ABOUT AN INCIDENT THAT HAD TAKEN PLACE A MONTH EARLIER, WHERE ANOTHER PHOTOJOURNALIST AND I HAD BEEN "PERMANENTLY BANNED" FOR TAKING PHOTOS OUTSIDE THE TRAIN STATION.

The ban was complete hogwash because there is no law prohibiting photography on the Metrorail, but a security guard took it upon himself to ban us, even after two police agencies had responded to the scene and discovered they had no grounds to arrest us—not that they didn't try.

I wrote about the first incident on my blog, including a video where the Homeland Security Bureau of the Miami-Dade Police Department ran our names into a terrorist watch list database to ensure we were not planning on blowing up the station after photographing it; this is part

of the absurdity photographers have had to face on a daily basis since the 9/11 terrorist attacks. That article and video went viral, which is how the news crew from HDNet, a satellite news network owned by Dallas Mavericks owner Mark Cuban, became interested in the story and flew in from Denver to interview me.

I invited the news crew to join me as I tried entering the station with a camera because I knew that in order for them to legally ban me from the station, they would have had to go through due process, which would have gone nowhere considering I had not broken any law. So after paying the fare, I walked into the station holding up a small video camera while HDNet reporter Greg Dobbs followed me inside and the camera crew remained outside recording the entry. Within seconds, a female security guard ordered me out of the station while a male security guard snuck up behind me and slapped the camera out of my hand, causing it to go flying to the floor. He then picked it up and pocketed it, refusing to give it back as he ordered me out of the station. I started snapping photos of the guards with my Canon 5D as they tried to force me out of the station before remembering I had my iPhone in my pocket, so I pulled it out and started video recording, embarrassingly in the vertical position as I was not accustomed to recording on my iPhone at the time—an annoying habit that every citizen journalist should refrain from doing.

I was refusing to leave on the basis that I had paid my fare, wasn't breaking any laws and they had illegally seized my camera, refusing to return it. It was a chaotic scene to say the least, especially considering the female security guard kept chasing after me while telling me to "get that camera out of my face" and the male guard started pushing me while telling me, "don't push me."

METRORAIL PROTEST, MIAMI, 2010

You can see the video by searching for "Metrorail security guard assaults me" on YouTube, dated July 29, 2010.

When the male security guard again tried to slap the camera out of my hand, I responded by punching him in the face. It was a very instinctive reaction and I regretted it immediately, and it's not something I would recommend ever doing, but sometimes things get out of control. The guard responded by pulling out a metal baton and coming after me, so I stepped out of the station without the camera they had confiscated from me. Police were called and there was discussion among the news crew as to whether I should leave considering there was a good chance I would be arrested for battery on the security guard. I decided to stay, maintaining that I was only defending myself after the guard had slapped my hand twice. And I didn't want to leave the scene without my camera.

Police and paramedics arrived on the scene within minutes, so while they took statements from the guards, I uploaded the video to Twitter from my iPhone, something I had never done before because I was always in the habit of using other video cameras that recorded in better quality but did not have the ability to upload directly to the internet. From Twitter, I posted the video on Facebook. And within minutes, the video began going viral. And as I sat there with Dobbs, a two-time Emmy-award-winning journalist who covered the 1979 Iranian revolution and the ensuing hostage crisis at the U.S. embassy as well as the Soviet invasion of Afghanistan—a man who has covered stories from all over the globe since the 1970s—I will never forget how impressed he was that my video was already making waves.

This is a man who had done it all, had seen it all, had covered it all. Yet there I was educating him about the power of social media. Ultimately, it was the footage on HDNet's camera that convinced police I had acted in self-defense. But it took two hours to sort it all out.

That night, I posted the video on my blog with a full write-up. And HDNet posted its footage next to my footage in a side-by-side video with their own write-up within a couple of days, so the story continued to go viral. However, social media gave me the opportunity to provide an instant on-the-scene report of what took place to my readers within minutes, a luxury that was limited to the giant news corporations only a few years earlier. Without social media, there would be no such thing as citizen journalism, so it's important to utilize it to our full advantage, which you learn how to do in the next few sections.

METRORAIL PROTEST, MIAMI, 2010

BUILDING ONLINE COMMUNITIES

WHEN I LAUNCHED MY BLOG IN APRIL 2007, I DID SO WITH THE INTENTION THAT I WOULD SHUT IT DOWN ONCE I WAS ACQUITTED OF ALL MY CHARGES, CONFIDENT THAT BY PUBLISHING THE PHOTO EVIDENCE ONLINE, THE PROSECUTORS WOULD HAVE NO CHOICE BUT TO DROP THE CHARGES.

But I learned that once you fight them in the court of public opinion, they will do all they can to prosecute you, despite photo evidence that proves your innocence, which in my case, was a photo that showed the street behind the officers, even though they claimed I was standing in the middle of the street before they arrested me.

Throw in a biased judge who was a former police union lawyer and it's not surprising I ended up convicted of resisting arrest, even though I was acquitted of the other charges.

Once I decided to appeal that conviction, which was followed by a second arrest for photographing cops against their wishes (and eventually a third), it became clear that my blog was not going to be as short-lived as I had initially envisioned. But it was my friend Eddie North-Hager who made me see the true potential of what I was creating, persuading me to start taking a more professional approach to my blog as opposed to just treating it as a side hobby. And it was North-Hager who made me see the value of creating an online community, which I now know is vital to the success of any independent journalist.

At the time, North-Hager was creating his own online community after launching a blog covering issues in his Los Angeles neighborhood—Leimert Park, in April 2007, the same month I launched PINAC. Today, he runs seven community blogs in Los Angeles, each of them with their own look, style, voice and writers. And he's looking to double that amount within two years.

"I have community partners in each neighborhood who help me manage the sites and content," he said. "These are professional writers. When we make a profit, they get a cut. But we don't always make a profit."

At the time of this writing, October 2013, he had almost 5,000 registered members on his sites, with hundreds of them regularly posting content.

"They are true citizen journalists," he said. "They don't have journalism training. They can write about the school play or question why their trash didn't get picked up."

VOTING RALLY, MIAMI, 2008

North-Hager and I became close friends after having worked at three different newspapers together. But like me, he became jaded with the business, so he ended up accepting a job in media relations at the University of Southern California, a move newspaper veterans have traditionally referred to as "going to the dark side." But the journalism bug is harder to shed than the job, so in 2007, he began pursuing a masters degree in online communities, a newly created program at the USC Annenberg School for Communication and Journalism. And one of his first assignments was to create an idea for an online community. He not only created an idea, he created an actual online community by launching a community blog covering his neighborhood in Los Angeles.

"Everybody in class turned in a Photoshopped version of what their front page would look like," he said. "I turned in an actual page."

What started out as a single neighborhood blog called *Leimert*

Park Beat: The Soul of Los Angeles is now a network of blogs covering various neighborhoods, each of them with their own voice and writers, titled *Rancho Park Online*, *Silver Lake Star*, *Echo Park Online*, *Culver City Times*, *University Park Family* and the *San Pedro News Pilot*.

"Anybody who signs up as a registered member has certain privileges where they can post blogs, events, photos and videos," he said. "Everybody is a potential writer. Everybody is a citizen journalist."

He views his websites as community newspapers with the difference that the voices and opinions are coming from the community.

"Newspapers report on how they viewed the event from an outsider's eye," he said. "I didn't want to do that with these sites because I was new to the community when I first launched the blog." However, it takes more than just launching a blog to make it work.

"You need to have a real world component," he said. "I became chaplain of my block club, and I am on the executive board of my neighborhood council."

It took two years to get Leimert Park Beat to where citizens were contributing on a regular basis, allowing him to turn his attention to launch a second site, which was around the time local businesses began contacting him to advertise. At the time of this writing, he makes enough to keep the sites going with a little extra for his wallet, but not enough to make a living. But he has seen the failures of newspapers and the failures of community sites, like *Patch*, that tried to do what he is doing, and believes he can make it work by prioritizing content and community over profit and proceeds.

"When you're publicly owned, you need to ensure a higher profit margin for your shareholders, but when you're privately owned, your overheads and expectations are different," he said.

The one thing we both learned in building our respective online communities is that the results are not immediate, but the bonds you create with your followers are a lot stronger than you would see between a corporate news site and its readers.

"It takes time to sow the seeds and have it bring fruit," he said.

COMMUNITY INVESTIGATION, 2012

SUTRO AVENUE BOOK CLUB, 2012

THE KINGDOM DAY, MARTIN LUTHER KING FESTIVAL, 2012

CROWDFUNDED JOURNALISM

JENNA POPE'S TRANSITION FROM CRIMINAL JUSTICE MAJOR TO GLOBETROTTING PHOTOJOURNALIST BEGAN WITH A SERIES OF PROTESTS INSIDE THE WISCONSIN STATE CAPITOL IN FEBRUARY 2011.

She was 20 years old and studying at the University of Wisconsin Milwaukee, planning on becoming a police officer. She was also a photographer but focusing mostly on portraits and weddings. But when Governor Scott Walker introduced a bill that would strip the collective bargaining power from public sector employees along with other budget cuts, she joined tens of thousands of other Wisconsinites in protesting against the passing of the bill.

After more than two weeks of protesting in Madison, the state's capital, she returned to Milwaukee, joining more than 70 other students in occupying a building on campus to protest against university budget cuts that were also included in what was known as the Wisconsin Budget Repair Bill. She then returned to Madison in the summer and continued protesting against Walker along with hundreds of others in what became an ongoing presence in the capital that year (and even later than

TAKSIM GEZI PARK, TURKEY, 2013

that after the bill was passed and after Walker was re-elected in a failed recall attempt).

By June of that year, Pope decided she no longer wanted to be a cop. In fact, she no longer wanted to be a student, realizing her passion was in activism. So when the Occupy Wall Street protesters set up their encampment in Lower Manhattan in September 2011, she and a videographer friend drove to New York with the intention of covering it

for Wisconsinites. And they paid for it all through crowdfunding, which is essentially asking their friends and followers to contribute through donations of any size, big or small.

It has proven to be a successful recipe for Pope, who has traveled to Turkey twice to cover the protests of 2013, as well as to Tampa and Charlotte to cover the national conventions in 2012. Along the way, she established herself as a professional photojournalist, becoming

a regular contributor to *The Real News Network* as well as selling an epic photo from the Republican National Convention that ended up on the cover of Radley Balko's book, *Rise of the Warrior Cop: The Militarization of America's Police Forces*, making her enough money to pay for her initial trip to Turkey, where she stayed for two weeks, producing enough content to raise her enough money through donations to pay for a second trip to Turkey later that summer. And through

CITIZEN PROFILE: JENNA POPE

it all, she was shot with water cannons and has dodged bullets to show the world what the Turkish government was trying its best to cover up.

"Turkey is the country with the most jailed journalists, so their media was not covering the protests," she said. "Even the journalists who wanted to cover it wouldn't because they were scared."

In fact, *The New York Times* reported that 72 Turkish journalists were fired for covering the protests, which began with a small sit-in demonstration against a planned demolition of a park before catapulting into a nationwide movement against various government injustices. Pope said the protests would have received little coverage had it not been for the influx of international journalists

as well as the local citizen journalists who posted videos and photos online. At a time when many American news companies have closed down foreign bureaus, the fact that she is willing to travel abroad to cover news is setting a new standard for citizen journalists. But it's not easy. She avoids hotels and even hostels, seeking places to sleep through her social media network.

TURKISH PROTESTOR, TAKSIM GEZI PARK, ISTANBUL, TURKEY, 2013

"I had posted on Facebook that I'm going to Turkey and I needed a place to stay and within a day, a friend of a friend of a friend invited me to stay at his place, which was about a seven-minute walk to Taksim Square (where much of the protests were centered)," she said.

She travels light, avoiding any large, bulky luggage that would have to checked in. But even then, she still manages to bring two DSLRs, one GoPro head cam, four lenses, a laptop computer as well as accessories, including a mobile hotspot, which is essential for uploading photos in the field. She also shuns traditional photo-editing programs like Photoshop and Lightroom, opting to use Pixlr, a free online photo editing program available at www.pixlr.com.

"While everybody else is going out for a drink, I'm on my laptop uploading photos," she said.

Her advice to anybody wishing to pursue their journalistic endeavors through crowdfunding?

"It takes a lot of time. It's not something where you can wake up and say, 'I want to be a full-time crowdfunded photographer.' I built my social media network for a year and a half before I even tried crowdfunding."

REPUBLICAN NATIONAL CONVENTION, CHARLOTTE, NC, USA, 2012

YOUTUBE

IN GIL SCOTT-HERON'S FAMOUS 1970 POEM, HE PROCLAIMED THAT THE REVOLUTION WILL NOT BE TELEVISED. AND HE WAS RIGHT. IT WILL INSTEAD BE BROADCAST OVER YOUTUBE AS WE'VE SEEN WITH VARIOUS PROTESTS, UPRISINGS AND REVOLTS OVER RECENT YEARS.

Facebook.com/WorldMustWakeUp

NSA Spying Through Online Video Games? Check out our latest video here

In fact, YouTube revolutionized citizen journalism more than any other medium. Before YouTube, publishing online video was restricted to the major news companies. It was still very new and burdensome to view, requiring users to download applications, and even then, most people were still using dial-up internet, which made watching video an exercise in patience, to say the least.

But that all changed in 2005 with the introduction of YouTube, which came around the time when more Americans began using broadband internet over dial-up. Even more revolutionary, YouTube allowed users to monetize their content, allowing users to make a very comfortable living as we can see in the case of Brian Bates, who is profiled in this book. But Bates had been shooting video for almost a decade earlier, so he already had the reputation, as well as an endless collection of videos to post. YouTube also allowed people with absolutely no prior journalistic experience to monetize on their content, truly democratizing journalism as never before.

Joel Franco was just fifteen years old when he first started making YouTube videos from his bedroom at his mom's apartment in Hialeah, a working-class suburb of Miami. His older brother had been talking to him about the Illuminati, and the related conspiracy theory stating that a shadowy group of elites secretly run the world. Whether you believe in it or not, there is no denying that it's a remarkably popular topic in online circles. So when Franco began making videos in 2009 on his YouTube channel, *World Must Wake Up*, he began developing a viewership.

But like many citizen journalists, the Occupy Wall Street movement became a huge turning point for him, which is when his videos began taking a more political tone.

"That's when I began to take my videos more seriously."

That was also when he began making $1,500 a month from his YouTube videos through the Google AdSense program, enabling him to buy a new laptop and DSLR, as well as give his mother $200 a month to help pay rent.

"For the first two years, I was just using a $130 point and shoot," he said.

At the time of this interview, he was 18 and preparing to graduate high school and enroll at Miami-Dade College to pursue a degree in journalism, which is exactly what I did two decades earlier. This is his advice to anybody wanting to making money on YouTube:

"You need to set aside time for it because it's very time-consuming," he said.

"I start out by searching the internet for the hottest stories, then do more fact checking on those stories, then set up the camera in my room to do a few takes, and then edit the video, and then post it on social media sites."

"It takes a large portion of my day to do it right."

But he knew he was doing it right when he started receiving messages from people overseas telling him to keep up the good work.

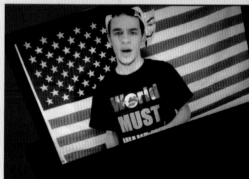

TWITTER

THE ANNOUNCEMENT THAT ORANGE COUNTY PROSECUTORS HAD RELEASED THE LONG-AWAITED VIDEO OF THE KELLY THOMAS BEATING BEGAN HITTING THE EAST COAST AT AROUND NOON ON MAY 7, 2012. AND BY THE DESCRIPTIONS COMING FROM REPORTERS, IT WAS GOING TO BE A GRUESOME VIDEO.

I had covered the gruesome story of Kelly Thomas extensively a year earlier, mainly from the angle of how Fullerton police officers had confiscated cameras from witnesses after beating the mentally ill homeless man to death. I had also written how police were refusing to release the city surveillance video that captured the beating in the parking lot of a bus depot. As I discuss in a case study in this book on pages 142-145, the Kelly Thomas beating received international attention only

CarlosMiller
@CarlosMiller FOLLOWS YOU
Writer, reporter, blogger, photojournalist, videographer, activist, rabble-rouser and truth-seeker.
Miami · photographyisnotacrime.com

11,625	739	3,655	
TWEETS	FOLLOWING	FOLLOWERS	Following

when a group of local citizen journalists began blogging about it, leading to several cops getting criminally charged with murder and manslaughter.

So now, almost a year after the beating, the Southern California media was out in full force, covering a court hearing in which the video was shown for the first time, assuring viewers they would run the video during their 5 p.m. newscasts, which would be 8 p.m. my time. I prepared to scoop the entire East Coast by creating a column on Twitter through Tweetdeck, a dashboard application that makes Twitter so much easier. I used the keywords, "Kelly Thomas video," knowing this would be much easier than searching multiple news sites for the video on Google.

The first results were from people in Southern California who had just seen the video on television; shocked, outraged responses that started flooding the newly created column on Tweetdeck. Knowing the video would soon be posted, I began writing the blog post, basing it on the descriptions from the reporters and tweeters. And within about fifteen minutes, it came across the Tweetdeck column from a local blog called *Fullerton Stories*.

I grabbed the embed code and posted it on my blog with a few short sentences before posting it on Facebook, Google+, and Twitter. I then proceeded to watch the video while updating the article with details, saving a new version about every five minutes, watching my story get continuously retweeted in the same column I had created. My story ended up receiving more than 125,000 views within 24 hours and more than 200,000

views in 48 hours, which was astronomical considering I was averaging less than 10,000 views a day at the time.

Twitter may not be the strongest platform to build an online community as everybody seems to be speaking into the wind, but nothing beats it when following a breaking news story, such as those that took place during the Occupy protests.

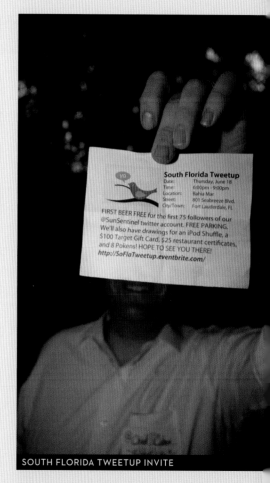

SOUTH FLORIDA TWEETUP INVITE

FACEBOOK

FOR THE FIRST THREE YEARS THAT I WAS RUNNING MY BLOG, I STUBBORNLY REFUSED TO LAUNCH A FACEBOOK "FAN PAGE," AS THEY WERE CALLED BACK THEN, EVEN THOUGH MY SOCIAL-MEDIA-SAVVY READERS AND FRIENDS CONSISTENTLY ENCOURAGED ME TO DO SO. I HAD BEEN BUILDING UP A READERSHIP THROUGH MY PERSONAL FACEBOOK PAGE, SO I SAW THE FAN PAGE AS BEING REDUNDANT, NOT TO MENTION THAT THE CONCEPT OF HAVING "FANS" SEEMED POMPOUS.

Nevertheless, in June 2010, one of my readers—a Boston photographer named Patrick Sullivan—took the liberty of creating a community page for me, which Facebook had introduced just a couple of months earlier to replace the earlier fan pages. However, I unintentionally neglected the page during the first year because I was so focused on building the readership on my personal Facebook page, always forgetting to post my stories on that page as well.

Despite that neglect, the *Photography is Not a Crime* Facebook page began growing on its own. Followers (no longer called "fans" by that point) primarily used it as a platform on which to post links and news tips for my blog. By the time it reached 1,500 likes, I realized I was sitting on a gold mine and started posting my stories on it as well as on my personal page.

As of early 2014, which is when I am writing this, the *Photography is Not a Crime* Facebook page has more than 17,000 likes, while I have 3,700 friends on my personal Facebook page along with 1,200 followers.

Even though I post with much more frequency on my personal page, those posts are often on topics that may not be related to my blog. The community page, though updated less frequently, is consistently on-topic, and has drawn much more followers in a much shorter time period. The lesson I learned was clear: People will follow a journalist's community page before they friend that journalist on his personal page, most likely because they don't personally know that journalist.

Everybody has different standards when it comes to Facebook. I accept pretty much any friendship as long as it's not obviously spam because I view Facebook as a networking platform and I would never post anything online that I wouldn't want the world to see. Others view it as a platform to share photos and life events with friends and families, treating it as a more intimate network, so it's understandable why they wouldn't want to accept a random friend invite just because that person enjoys their blog. By liking the *Photography is Not a Crime* page, they can follow my journalism stories without having to share any personal details about their lives. So it is highly recommended to create a community page to expand your audience as only about 5% of my followers on the community page follow me on my personal page, proving my original assumption of redundancy flat wrong. It's also worth noting that Facebook gives admins of dedicated community pages a suite of analytical tools to help see how far their posts are reaching, which can help curate content.

AFTERMATH OF A TORNADO IN PLEASANT GROVE, ALABAMA, 2011

GOOGLE+

LIKE MANY OF MY SOCIAL MEDIA PEERS IN SOUTH FLORIDA, I HOPPED ON THE GOOGLE+ BANDWAGON AFTER IT LAUNCHED IN 2011 WITH MANY PREDICTING IT WOULD REPLACE FACEBOOK. AND LIKE MOST OF THEM, I DIDN'T INVEST THE TIME TO FIGURE OUT HOW TO FULLY UTILIZE GOOGLE+, USING IT TO POST MY ARTICLES, BUT NOTHING MORE, WHILE SPENDING THE BULK OF MY SOCIAL MEDIA TIME ON FACEBOOK, WHERE I HAD DEVELOPED A VERY ACTIVE ONLINE COMMUNITY.

Carlos Miller
Works at Photography is Not a Crime
Attended Florida International University
Lives in Miami

Add to circles

6,407 have him in circles

About **Posts** Photos YouTube Reviews

I quickly developed a following on Google+ because of my blog. More than 6,000 people put me in their circles, which is how people follow each other on this platform. However, I didn't make much of an effort to interact with followers by placing them in my circles, which resulted in my blog getting very little page views from the platform.

That, in itself, is a lesson in social media and online communities: The more you interact, the more your work will get noticed; the less you interact, the less your work will be noticed.

This is a lesson that has failed most mainstream reporters who have grown so accustomed to being the sole communicators to a captive audience that we all know has become much less captive in recent years because of the rising number of options on the internet.

In researching this topic, I reached out to my friend, Cynthia K. Seymour, who runs a Miami consulting company called www.seymourresults.com, and has become a Google+ guru. I expected to do the typical phone interview, but she suggested we do a Google Hangout where we would be able to talk face to face through our computers. The interview lasted over an hour and you can view it by searching for "Carlos Miller Chats with Cynthia K Seymour about G+." That, in itself, was a prime example of how Google+ can benefit citizen journalists; the ability to conduct face-to-face interviews with anybody in the world and have it automatically posted on YouTube within minutes.

Seymour, along with co-host Debbie Elicksen, host a weekly show on Google+ called *Virtual Newsmakers* where they interview interesting people from around the world, including me—you can see the interview by googling "Virtual Newsmakers features Carlos Miller, Photography Is Not A Crime."

Seymour provided a number of reasons why Google+ is the best social media platform for citizen journalists, the main reason being that Google pretty much owns the internet, so your content will

be prioritized over other platforms. But she also emphasized how a simple Google Hangout interview can lead to various forms of content, beginning with a YouTube video that not only can be monetized, but also embedded in a blog as well as transcribed for a blog with screenshots from the video as images.

"Then you can strip it down into a podcast, that's another kind of content," she said. "Then you can take it into tweets, that's another type of content."

By the time the interview was over, I was completely sold on Google+, assuring Seymour that I would take the 90-day challenge to prioritize it over Facebook, so hopefully by the time you read this, I will be conducting my own Google Hangouts with photo rights activists from around the world.

G20 PROTESTS, TORONTO, CANADA, 2010

THE LAST KISS

IN AUGUST 2012, AT THE AGE OF 42, MO GELBER WAS THREE YEARS INTO OWNING A DIGITAL DSLR, A SELF-TRAINED TRAVEL AND STREET PHOTOGRAPHER WITH ASPIRATIONS OF BECOMING A NEWSPAPER PHOTOJOURNALIST, WHEN HE CAME ACROSS A MOB OF TELEVISION AND NEWSPAPER REPORTERS STANDING OUTSIDE A POLICE PRECINCT IN LOWER MANHATTAN.

As always, he had his camera with him, strapped to his neck, no longer carrying it in a camera bag because he had learned those extra 15 seconds could make the difference in nailing a perfect shot. The audio systems engineer strode up to the media frenzy, trying to blend in, realizing it was a press conference for Anna Gristina, the "Millionaire Madam" who ended up convicted of running a brothel that catered to New York City's power elite. Standing outside the crowd, he stood on a pillar with his Canon Rebel T2i and 70-200 f/4 lens and started shooting Gristina, her attorney, and the reporters shoving microphones in their faces.

That was when he noticed two police officers down the street escorting a handcuffed couple, the man appearing to lean towards the woman for a kiss as the officers maintained a grip on their arms. Gelber turned his camera towards the foursome and snapped away, capturing the shot that he would title, "The Last Kiss." He posted the photo on Facebook, as he had done hundreds of times before, but this time, the photo started going viral immediately, receiving more than 100,000 likes within the first few hours after it was shared hundreds of times. He then entered the photo in the Project Imaginat1on photo contest, sponsored by filmmaker Ron Howard and Canon, in which the winning photo would be turned into a short film. Within days, he received a call informing him that his photo was one of the finalists out of hundreds of entries. But before the photo could go any further in the

suspects without a name, considering they arrests hundreds of people daily.

So Gelber reposted the photo on Facebook, asking his friends and followers to help track down the couple so he could have them sign the release. And before he knew it, the photo started going viral again, but this time, it was picked up by local and national media, not only intrigued by the photo, but wanting to help track the couple down.

The woman in the picture, Alexis Creque, was tracked down the following day, reaching out to Gelber to tell him she would only sign the release, if her boyfriend, Russell Murphy, would sign it. Murphy had been arrested for spray painting graffiti on a building. Creque had been arrested for being his lookout. She had been released but he had been kept in jail. In the end, the couple did not sign the release under the advice of their attorney, who was not happy at all the publicity her client was receiving. But the publicity gained Gelber hundreds more followers, as well as an

contest, he needed to obtain model releases from each of the subjects, including the two suspects and two NYPD officers. And he had less than three days to do so.

"I said, 'sure, no problem,' but then hung up the phone realizing I didn't know who these people were," he recalled in a telephone interview.

He zoomed in on the name tags and badge numbers of the police officers and was able to track them down through a buddy who works for the NYPD, finding out that one officer agreed to sign it, but the other officer was away on vacation. However, police tracked her down and she faxed a signed release form from Virginia. But police weren't able to track down the

CITIZEN PROFILE: MO GELBER

assignment with the *New York Daily News*, a step closer to his goal of becoming a newspaper photojournalist.

Less than two months later, after almost daily postings of New York City street photography to his Facebook page, Hurricane Sandy struck New York City, leaving widespread flooding throughout much of the boroughs, including Manhattan's financial district. The media naturally stuck to covering Manhattan and ignoring the outer boroughs, especially the hard-hit area of the Rockaway Peninsula in Queens, about 25 miles from the city's financial district. The area was struck so badly that there was no running water or electricity and all the streets were blocked off with debris and trees, leaving residents isolated from the core of the city. Gelber, who lives in Brooklyn, rode his bicycle down to the stricken area with his camera, and began taking photos of the devastation before residents started inviting him into their homes, wanting to show them the damage and tell their stories because nobody from the government had been out there to help them. So he would spend hours taking

photos, posting their stories on Facebook and letting the world know about their plight.

"I was doing a lot of reporting, which is different than the hit-and-run style of street photography I normally do," he said. "I was hoping that by reporting it, the city agencies would take notice and help them.

"It took them like a week to finally make it out there."

He realizes getting such a late start in photography makes it hard for him to get hired at a newspaper, especially at a time when newspapers are laying off their entire photo staffs.

"I have a passion for photography that I think many newspaper photojournalists have lost," he said.

ON THE BEAT

THE FIRST TIME I HELD A SINGLE-LENS REFLEX CAMERA WAS AFTER I WAS HIRED AT MY FIRST FULL-TIME NEWSPAPER JOB IN 1997, AFTER SPENDING ALMOST A YEAR AS A PART-TIME FEATURES WRITER AT THE *TUCSON CITIZEN*.

The *Deming Headlight*, a small newspaper in Southern New Mexico near the Mexican border, didn't have a staff photographer, so the reporters (all three of us) were required to take our own photos with our stories. At the time, my only camera experience was taking snapshots with a point and shoot, so it was a little overwhelming when they handed me a Minolta XG-1—a no-nonsense, manual-focus film SLR (to its credit, at least it did have an automatic exposure mode). I was not only limited to a single 50mm lens, the newspaper did not have a flash to go

with the camera—not even the build-in type that we all take for granted today.

I ended up checking out all the books about photography from the local library, learning everything I could about composition, lighting, exposure, and speed, as we didn't even have the internet yet. Now, photography takes years to master (some would say a lifetime), and I'm not even close to that level of skill as I write this, but I was motivated and enthusiastic enough that you can be it didn't take very long for me to learn the fundamentals.

Within a year, I switched jobs to the larger newspaper in the area, the *Las Cruces Sun-News*, and my father bought me a fantastic birthday present: a Canon Elan IIe (called the EOS 50 in Europe). This was a serious camera, packed with features—not the least of which was, you guessed it, autofocus. He even threw in a couple of zoom lenses with the package. They may have been entry-level lenses, but suddenly I had more than a single focal length, and didn't have to zoom with my feet everywhere I went. I was hooked.

And throughout the rest of my newspaper career, which took me to the *San Bernardino Sun* and the *Arizona Republic* before I moved back to Miami, I was known as a reporter who took photos—a rarity in those days when the newsrooms were filled with either photojournalists or reporters, most who were unable to do both.

After my first arrest, which prompted me to launch my blog, I learned how to shoot video when I saw the impact YouTube was making on the internet.

Today, I call myself a "multimedia journalist" because I not only write, take photos and shoot video, I publish it all to the Web. I am a one-man newsroom, which is what we all have to be these days.

Julie Dermansky, who is profiled on pages 78–81, started off as a photographer, but then became a videographer and a writer after realizing that's the key to selling content to news sites. She has now been published in countless sites, earning regular checks for her articles, photos and videos.

"I learned that if you pitch the photo editor cold, you will get nowhere, but if you pitch the editors at the news desk, they will listen if you have photos and a story idea," she says.

BP OIL SPILL, LOUISIANA, 2010

LESSONS FROM A PRO

GEO RODRIGUEZ

AFTER SPENDING SIX YEARS IN TEXAS WRITING FOR THE SAN ANTONIO EXPRESS-NEWS, IHOSVANI "GEO" RODRIGUEZ WAS EXCITED TO BE COMING BACK HOME FOR A DREAM JOB, WORKING THE POLICE BEAT FOR THE SOUTH FLORIDA *SUN SENTINEL* OUT OF THE MIAMI BUREAU.

"Having the opportunity to be a police reporter in Miami, my hometown and Edna Buchanan's old beat, was something I had always fantasized about since I was blown away by her book, *The Corpse Had a Familiar Face,* back in high school," he said. "It was the first book I had ever read in one sitting, and one of the very few I've gone back to read again over the years. So when I was offered the job, I didn't even ask how much."

Buchanan, a *Miami Herald* cop reporter during the crime-ridden 1980s, renowned for her sarcastic, punchy ledes, was also who inspired me to get into journalism, so I understood where Rodriguez was coming from. It was 2004 and the Fort Lauderdale-based Sun Sentinel was making a foray into neighboring Miami to compete head-to-head against the rival *Miami Herald,* which had long been the state's dominant newspaper. But when the economy tanked in 2007, the *Sun Sentinel* shut down its bureau, leaving Rodriguez without a beat.

He began covering Hollywood, a city in Broward County, but in 2008, a content-sharing agreement between the *Miami Herald,* the *Sun Sentinel,* and the *Palm Beach Post* determined it would be covered by the *Herald*, not only leaving him without a beat again, but killing the competition that had brought Rodriguez back home in the first place. And considering the *Sentinel* was in the process of laying off 20% of its newsroom, he was thinking he would soon be out of a job, ending his journalism career at the age of 38.

That was also the year when the Tribune Company, owner of the *Sun Sentinel*, combined the newspaper's operations with a South Florida television station it owned in order to cut back on resources. That gave Rodriguez the opportunity to learn how to shoot video, something he had never done before; something most news reporters would never dare do.

"They gave me no training so I had to learn it all myself," he said. "But it saved my career because that was when everybody was getting laid off."

Over the next two years, Rodriguez became a multimedia journalist, meaning he would shoot and edit video as well as write stories, a rarity

EDNA BUCHANAN

GEO SKYDIVING WITH THE U.S. ARMY GOLDEN KNIGHTS, 2010

in the mainstream media, but becoming much more common these days out of necessity.

It's a lesson that can be applied to all citizen journalists considering we are living in the age of the one-man newsroom. And it's a lesson that can be applied to all corporate journalists who never know when they will be laid-off.

By 2010, Rodriguez was being flown around the country to teach reporters at the Tribune's other newspapers on how to become videographers, even writing a short manual with solid pointers—shown on the opposite page.

The 10-page PDF titled Geo's *Video Guide* can be found on my site, www.photographyisnotacrime.com, by searching for "Ten Rules for Recording Cops (and Other Authority Figures)," linked towards the bottom. It is recommended reading, even if you've been shooting for a while, because it doesn't hurt to get a refresher course in basic video photojournalism. And if you're a beginner, it's essential reading

because they are tips you will eventually learn along the way through trial and error, just as Rodriguez and I did, so might as well learn them now. But he's learned a lot more since publishing the guide, especially when it comes to video length.

"You really don't want to go over two minutes unless the video is very compelling because that's when human attention spans begin to wander," he said, adding that his newspaper has done analytical studies to confirm this.

"You also want to put the most compelling part of the video in the beginning, just like you would when writing a good lede."

This is actually a literary technique with an illustrious history going all the way back to the Greek epics, and which the Romans dubbed *en media res*, meaning to start in the middle of the story, at the height of the action. And in today's fast-paced world, that technique is even more important to grab viewers before they become bored and click away.

One of my biggest gripes with citizen journalists is that they make their videos too long, not bothering to edit the boring parts out, even if it forces the viewer to spend three minutes to get to the point where something happens. Please stop doing that.

Rodriguez also stressed the importance of B-roll footage, which is the footage you shoot that may be secondary to an interview or the main action you are shooting, but can be supplemented into the video during editing to make for a more compelling video.

"You really don't want to be sitting there while editing and say, 'I should have shot that,'" he said.

He also emphasized the importance of audio, whether it is audio from an interview, a music band, a passing train, or horn blasts that you may be able to use as background sound over other clips to make a more compelling video. To ensure optimal sound quality, he recommends wearing headphones, which will enable you to pick up on any distracting sounds you may not hear otherwise, like a noisy air conditioner, highway traffic or chirping birds. And last but not least, get into the habit of using a tripod, as burdensome as it may be to carry it around. Because even if you do capture clear sound and plenty of B-roll, your video is still going to look unprofesional if it's shaky and wobbly.

GEO, ON HIS BEAT

GEO'S VIDEO GUIDE

A straightforward guide to shooting video, specifically tailored for reporters and citizen journalists.

THE VIDEO VIGILANTE

BRIAN BATES MOVED TO OKLAHOMA CITY'S CLASSEN TEN-PENN NEIGHBORHOOD IN 1996 TO TAKE A MARKETING JOB AT A NEARBY HOSPITAL. IT DIDN'T TAKE HIM LONG TO REALIZE THAT HE HAD MOVED INTO A NEIGHBORHOOD RAMPANT WITH PROSTITUTION.

And it wasn't something the 26-year-old man was happy with, so he reached out to police and neighborhood associations to put a stop to it. However, he never got anywhere. He even went as far as filing a complaint against a prostitute and her customer, testifying against them in court, but that also went nowhere because he had no proof.

So one day as he was sitting in traffic, behind three men in three different cars who were talking to three different prostitutes, he realized he had his Sharp Viewcam digital camcorder with him, which he would use for work-related events. He ended up following one of the men, who are commonly referred to as "johns," and waited for him to park his car on a side street. He surprised the man and the woman in the car by opening the door and videotaping them in the midst of a sexual act. He then tracked down a local police officer who

had the prostitute arrested. He turned in his footage to the local media and police and was immediately dubbed "The Video Vigilante"—a name he still proudly boasts today—even though he resisted it for years.

"I fought against it and refused to be interviewed if they called me that," he

said. "Eventually, I gave up because that fight was too distracting and I found the Video Vigilante moniker actually gave me some anonymity."

For the next several years, Bates became a local celebrity by regularly following the johns, watching them as they parked in alleyways and parking lots and open fields to engage in sex before sneaking up on them and opening the car doors and boldly announcing his trademark phrase: "You're busted, buddy!"

In 2002, as the internet became more mainstream and the creation of personal websites became more accessible, Bates launched a website consisting mostly of photos because it was still very difficult and costly at the time to upload videos. But that all changed in October 2006, a year after the launching of YouTube, where he quickly became a star with the introduction of his channel, *Oklahoma City's Own Video Vigilante*. He already had ten years' worth of videos, plus he was frequently recording more, so he was never lacking for content.

He became so popular that YouTube invited him to join its Partner Program when it launched it in May 2007, allowing him to place ads on his videos, which generated income. And from there, he began licensing his videos to *Dateline*, 20/20, and the *Maury Povich Show*, the latter who gave him a lucrative contract to provide steady content for the show's "Caught on Tape" series.

"After that, I didn't have to work a real job again," he said.

CITIZEN PROFILE: BRIAN BATES

But his work has never been short of controversy and danger. In fact, over the years, he's been shot at, maced, and chased on foot by angry pimps. He's also been arrested and charged with pandering and aiding and abetting prostitution. That's right, the man who spent years exposing prostitutes caught in the act was accused of paying them to set up the acts.

That was back in 2005, a case that had him facing 140 years in prison before it was dismissed on a technicality without it even making it to trial. Bates said it was a setup by an overzealous prosecutor who wanted to retaliate against him for having embarrassed him years earlier.

In July 2002, Bates followed a man who had picked up a prostitute before parking in a church parking lot where they both made their way into the back of a covered truck. At the time, he had a great relationship with the Oklahoma

City Police Department because he gave them great exposure when they would arrest the prostitutes and johns he would catch on camera. But that would all change on this day after Bates video recorded a couple of white cops beating a black man as they tried to handcuff him. Bates stood back recording the encounter as the officer drew his weapon, pointed it at the man and told him, "I will f__ing shoot you right in the head." The officer, joined by a second officer, then proceeded to beat Donald Pete with batons for several minutes as they tried to handcuff him while Bates continued recording what became a racially charged national controversy.

In trying to justify his decision not to charge the officers with excessive force, Oklahoma County District Attorney Wes Lane used Bates' video—muting the officer's threat to Pete about shooting him in the head—before showing it at a press conference. Rather than remain silent about it, Bates called his own press conference, allowing the media to hear what the cop had really said.

"I embarrassed him" Bates said. "I caught him in a lie. We became mortal enemies after that."

After this episode, Lane embarked on a campaign to have Bates imprisoned, relying on a statement from a prostitute (whose own mother claimed she was lying) that Bates had paid her to set up sex encounters with men so he could catch them in the act on video. Lane's crusade against Bates ended up costing him the election.

VIGILANTE JUSTICE?

As I say, there's no shortage of controversy in Bates' line of work. It's certainly more focused form of citizen journalism; he has a particular mission and has come to make a living off of it—much like a photographer will focus his skills over the course of his career and end up concentrating on one particular genre, or indeed, the way a journalist develops a speciality and a particular topic. Illegal prostitution was bound to be a contentious topic to focus on, but the key is that Bates has done his due diligence—he's researched the law, keeping in regular touch with the police, and made his motives very clear. He's worked hard to build up a reputation of legitimacy, and that applies regardless of your subject.

PUBLIC RECORDS

POLICE RECORDS OFFICE, HIALEAH, FLORIDA, 2013

A FEW WEEKS AFTER MY THIRD ARREST, MY ATTORNEY, ARNOLD TREVILLA, DEPOSED MIAMI-DADE POLICE MAJOR NANCY PEREZ TO INQUIRE AS TO WHY SHE ARRESTED ME DURING THE OCCUPY MIAMI EVICTION WHEN SHE DIDN'T ARREST THE GROUP OF CORPORATE JOURNALISTS WHO WERE ALSO COVERING THE EVICTION.

Perez, a public information officer, told Trevilla that she just assumed I was an activist, not a journalist. And that I had been arrested for failing to disperse after the activists had been ordered to do so. She also assured him that she had no idea who I was prior to the arrest, only later realizing that I ran a popular national blog when the news of my arrest and subsequent recovery of my deleted video footage made national headlines. But then, brothers Joel and Robert Chandler, a pair of public records experts from Central Florida, who were also avid readers of

my blog, made a public records request to the Miami-Dade Police Department, asking for all internal emails containing my name from the day of my arrest onward. Those emails not only proved that Perez had received an email hours before my arrest, informing her exactly who I was (complete with my picture which they plucked from Facebook) but also that the department's Homeland Security Bureau had been monitoring my Facebook page all along, which was a little disturbing considering all I've ever done was try to hold police accountable for their actions.

It's no secret that the government monitors activists and journalists who openly question governmental policies, so we can do the same to them through public records requests. In fact, you might be surprised at just how much information is available through public records requests, although you probably wouldn't be surprised at just how difficult public officials will make it for you to obtain those records. But the internet has made it easy for us to learn about public records laws because not only are the laws usually posted online, each state also usually has a non-profit organization whose mission is to educate the public about these laws, which can easily found on Google by typing in a few keywords. And most states' public records law stipulate that we are not only allowed to inspect the public records, but we are also allowed to photograph them, which is why Joel Chandler and I got into the habit of walking into public agencies with our cameras recording to document our request.

But we have only done this at the local level where there are no laws prohibiting videography inside public buildings as long as it is done in areas where people have no expectation of privacy.

Federal regulations allow videography inside federal buildings for news purposes in entrances, lobbies, auditoriums, and foyers but require that you get permission from government agents before recording them, which shouldn't be that hard to do if you remain professional and stress that you just want to get your request on the record. And even if they don't

consent, you can still get the request on camera as long as you don't get them on camera. Capturing the request on camera also allows you to share the video with your followers to educate them on public records laws, creating even more citizen journalists in the process because that is the surest way to ensure government transparency. However, you must be prepared for resistance not only to your request itself, but also to your insistence on recording your request, and the complete encounter.

Many times, state and local agencies will tell you that you have to fill out a form or provide them with identification, which is not required by law in many states. For example, if you want to simply inspect the visitor's log, a clerk should hand it over and allow you to inspect and photograph it without further complications. But if you are requesting public records that may require a little research, then it's best to put it in writing to ensure nothing gets lost in translation. Although the law is on your side when it comes to

recording your public records request, there is no guarantee they won't call the police on you as they did to us in September 2013, which you can view by searching on Google for "we were detained by Hialeah police for making a public records request at city hall."

Hialeah is a municipality in Miami-Dade County renowned for its corruption and

felonious mayors, so it wasn't surprising that they took exception to us demanding a little transparency. But not only did we not get arrested, our story went viral, which made Hialeah the laughing stock of the internet for a couple of days. And one of my readers, Theo Karantsalis, followed it up with another public records request of the dispatch recordings where the mayor called the police on us, claiming

HIALEAH, FLORIDA, 2013

we were causing a disturbance, along with the city hall surveillance video that showed we were not causing a disturbance. The mayor and his chief of staff also claimed that we were refusing to leave, when our own videos confirmed we were never asked to leave, only leaving when it became clear they were not going to provide us the public records.

With so many resources on the internet, it shouldn't take long to learn the various laws regarding public records at the state and federal levels. The real challenge is remaining assertive when they deny you these records because we must never forget that these are our public records. The government is only the custodian of these records.

CAMERAS IN THE COURTROOM

COUNTY COURTHOUSE, MIAMI, 2012

OVER THE YEARS, I'VE WRITTEN ABOUT SEVERAL PEOPLE WHO HAVE BEEN ARRESTED FOR TRYING TO BRING A CAMERA INTO A COURTROOM OR PULLING OUT A CAMERA DURING A HEARING AND ATTEMPTING TO RECORD.

All of them claimed their First Amendment rights were violated, not realizing that First Amendment rights are not absolute in a courtroom where somebody's Sixth Amendment right to a fair trial is at stake. But if you do a little research, you may learn that you are able to enter a courtroom with a camera providing you meet certain guidelines, varying from state to state. Florida, for example, has some of the most liberal rules when it comes to bringing cameras into the courtrooms, which was why I was able to bring in a videographer to record my third trial without going through any formal process, much to the detriment of the prosecuting team that tried to argue against it. The judge simply asked that we not record the jury to which we agreed.

Earlier that week, I had tested the Florida courtroom law by entering a hearing with my camera and tripod where a local blogger was being sued for defamation, deciding at the last minute to cover it as I had covered the case a few months earlier. The plaintiff's attorney, a Florida hotshot attorney named Alan Kluger, tried his best to get me tossed out, claiming I needed to file a written request beforehand (that's him waving and pointing on the opposite page). But the judge sided with the law, allowing me to remain as long as I refrained from moving around or changing lenses, which is a very reasonable request and included in the court rules regarding photography. You can see the video and story by searching for "Florida Attorney Alan Kluger Proves Not to Know Law Regarding Cameras in Courtrooms." The key as a citizen journalist is to understand that corporate journalists have been bringing in cameras into the courtrooms for years, so you just need to follow the procedures they've been doing because you have just as much right to record a hearing as they do. That said, courtrooms generally restrict the cameras to a single still camera and a single video camera, both of which much serve as a pool photographer to other media if the case is that high-profile. But these days, the media rarely covers the courts, much less sends photographers in to cover trials, so you can pretty much turn that into your own niche if you wish. Cameras are allowed in courtrooms in all 50 states, but the rules are not always the same, so do your research first and go through the proper procedures to ensure your right to record a hearing without getting arrested. It's worth noting, however, that in federal courtrooms, cameras are banned with few exceptions. But even that might eventually change as the federal courts have been experimenting with a pilot program, allowing cameras in certain courtrooms to see if the media's First Amendment right to record doesn't interfere with a defendant's Sixth Amendment right to a fair trial.

ME, IDENTIFYING MYSELF

THE GLOBETROTTING JOURNALIST

WITH THE EYE OF AN ARTIST AND THE HUSTLE OF A NEW YORKER—AND ABSOLUTELY NO JOURNALISTIC BACKGROUND OR TRAINING—JULIE DERMANSKY TOSSED ASIDE ALMOST TWO DECADES AS A SUCCESSFUL MANHATTAN ARTIST TO BECOME A PROFILIC JOURNALIST.

From a five-month stint embedded with the U.S. military in Iraq in 2008, to an impromptu trip to Haiti after the 2010 earthquake where she scored an exclusive interview with former presidents Bill Clinton and George W. Bush, to an 18-hour plane trip to Egypt during the Arab Spring uprising where she had her DSLRs confiscated at the airport—still managing to smuggle in a point-and-shoot—Dermansky has done more since 2008 than most corporate journalists have done in a lifetime. And she's only getting started.

"At first, I didn't know much about journalism," she said. "I just met people and started talking to them."

It's a simple rule. A very basic rule. Especially for journalists. But it's a rule that has been lost in this cyber era of social media detachment and emails that never get returned. It's also a rule that has set Dermansky apart from most modern-day journalists who prefer to communicate electronically.

"You look up the number to the publication and get the secretary, then ask to talk to the national desk, then you tell them what you got."

From a photographer, she became a writer and a videographer because she discovered that it's much easier to sell comprehensive multimedia packages than just photos alone.

Dermansky's story starts in New York in 1990 where she started off as an artist selling jewelry on the streets, running from the cops because she didn't have

TAHRIR SQUARE, DAY AFTER PRESIDENT MUBAREK STEPPED DOWN, CAIRO, EGYPT, 2011

the proper vendor's license. But it didn't take long before she was selling her jewelry to one of New York City's most famous bookstores. She then switched from making jewelry to welding furniture and home accessories and fine art, which also became a successful commercial venture. But things got hectic in the city so she bought a farmhouse more than two hours outside New York City for privacy, where she continued her business.

And then came the transition that would have her traveling the world, selling photos, videos and articles to *The Atlantic*, *US News*, the *Telegraph*, *The Guardian*, *The Times of London*, *The New York Times*, *The Washington Post*, *NPR*, and many more. In 2005, after a tornado demolished her farmhouse, she used her insurance money to embark on a global dark tourism project, photographing places of genocide and social injustice, a topic that has always interested her, spending the next year in Rwanda, South Africa, Egypt, Uganda, Ethiopia, Mauritius, Hong Kong, Cambodia, Vietnam and China, before ending up in Los Angeles.

CITIZEN PROFILE: JULIE DERMANSKY

In 2006, she landed in New Orleans, one year after Hurricane Katrina flooded and demolished most of the city, spending days walking the city and talking to survivors who were left with nothing, taking photographs that eventually ended up as an exhibit in the Chicago Field Museum.

But her "jump into journalism" didn't come until 2008 when she joined her documentary videographer boyfriend on a government-funded, military-embedded trip to Iraq, which isn't as hard to get as it sounds.

"The key is to get a local TV station to vouch for you," she said.

And it didn't hurt that she had made extensive contacts with the National Guard after partaking in three months of ride-alongs with them as they patrolled the streets of New Orleans long after Katrina.

"You have to meet the movers and shakers, you call people in logistics, you contact the public affairs officer," she said. She returned to New Orleans in 2009. When a friend died in the 2010 Haiti earthquake, she called her military contacts, telling them she wanted to cover it. "They said, 'Can you be ready in 24 hours?'" she remembered. She said, yes, of course, she was born ready. Ten days later, she was in Haiti, sleeping on a runway with the military and her Canon DSLRs. When she heard former presidents Bush and Clinton had flown in to survey the damage, she jumped on the back of a motorcycle with a photographer from the United Nations and ended up interviewing both of them, selling the videos to *The Atlantic*.

In February 2011, while vacationing in the Bahamas, her first vacation in an eternity, she was keeping up with the blossoming Arab Spring protests in the Middle East, especially the growing unrest in Cairo where she had a friend.

After contacting her friend, who confirmed she was allowed to stay at his place, she booked a flight and left the following day. But Egyptian customs officials confiscated her rolling bag of professional camera gear along with

PORT-AU-PRINCE, HAITI, 2010

the camera gear of every reporter flying into Cairo. Expecting this would happen, she had hidden a Flip camera and a point and shoot in a Wet Wipes container, which she ended up using to sell photos and videos to *The Atlantic*.

So it was only natural for her to jump on a plane from New Orleans to New York City when the Occupy Wall Street protests heated up after the infamous pepper spray incident, which you will read about in the Occupy Wall Street

case study. And after a few weeks of covering that, she flew to Oakland to cover the Occupy movement, and the following year to Chicago to cover the NATO protests.

The artist-turned-journalist is also a stout environmentalist, so in 2013, she became a regular contributor to the DeSmogBlog, which describes itself as "the world's number one source for accurate, fact-based information regarding global warming

misinformation campaigns." She admits she's not getting rich, but she's not going broke either, so she has no intention of stopping her journalism.

"I make just enough to pay the minimum amount of taxes," she said.

IRAQI POLICE LEARNING WEAPONS-HOLDING, IRAQ, 2008

AMERICAN SOLDIER, IRAQ, 2008

GOING PRO

PINAC

ABOUT A YEAR AFTER I FIRST LAUNCHED MY BLOG, I BECAME INVOLVED WITH THE SOCIAL MEDIA SCENE IN SOUTH FLORIDA, WHICH AT THAT TIME CONSISTED OF A GROUP OF LOCAL BLOGGERS AS WELL AS PEOPLE ON FACEBOOK AND TWITTER.

I would attend functions where speakers would rave about the benefits of "branding," a term I was highly skeptical of because it seemed like a marketing term. And marketing is an area of communications that I was always taught to steer clear away from if I wanted to maintain any degree of credibility as a journalist. So I wasn't immediately sold on the concept of branding myself as a journalist. But times have changed.

In today's social media blizzard where everybody is shouting into the wind,

it is absolutely necessary for journalists to brand themselves in order to set themselves apart. After all, major news organizations have been branding themselves for years, so it only makes sense for independent journalists do the same.

However, the mere mention of journalists branding themselves is enough to send other, more established journalists into a rant as we can see in Gene Weingarten's 2011 column in *The Washington Post* (Google keywords: "how branding is ruining journalism"):

Now, the first goal seems to be self-promotion—the fame part, the "brand." That's because we know that, in this frenetic fight for eyeballs at all costs, the attribute that is most rewarded is screeching ubiquity, not talent. It is why Snooki—who is quite possibly literally a moron—has a best-selling book. It is why the media superstars of today are no longer people such as Bob Woodward, who break big stories, but people like Bill O'Reilly, who yell about them.

He does have a point but as independent journalists, we don't always have the luxury of submitting our content to a news organization that will publish, promote and popularize our content, so we must do it all ourselves.

Besides, branding does not necessarily mean marketing, although it has always been a strong component of successful marketing campaigns.

In journalism, branding means being authentic, genuine and transparent in order to build a solid reputation. It also means creating a niche, a style, an expertise and allowing your personal voice to shine through, something traditional journalists have always been told not to do.

Branding is about building a rapport with your followers, which is essential in building an online community. It's about showing your personal side along with your professional side. But don't get too personal because you don't want people to forget you're a journalist.

It's simply keeping it real, which may or may not be different than how branding applies to marketing, which probably depends on the product being branded. In other words, don't be afraid to state your political ideology. Don't be afraid to state your religious beliefs. Don't be afraid to state your preference for greasy hamburgers.

But unless you're covering politics, religion or food, you don't want to obsess about these topics either. And you certainly don't want to censor

opposing opinions as long as they are civil. Most importantly, don't be afraid to show your value, but be smart enough not to overhype yourself.

As a citizen journalist, the first step in branding is establishing a social media presence. There are many platforms out there and while it's nice to use as many of them as you can, you run the danger of spreading yourself thin where it is impossible to build a successful brand.

After launching my blog, my goal was to earn respect from the mainstream media at a time when they didn't show much respect to the blogosphere. I also wanted to show the world that I was not afraid to state my opinion, which went against my corporate journalistic background where I was forced to be objective. At the time, many bloggers were in the habit of using pseudonyms or simply just going by their first name in order to retain a sense of privacy; I made sure to post my first and last name with every blog post I wrote to show that I stood behind everything I wrote. I told myself that I would never

say anything online that I wouldn't say in person, which fortunately, gave me a lot of leeway.

My goal was to combine my old-media experience with new-media technology. I remember telling my friend, Eddie North-Hager (see pages 42–45), that I wanted my blog to be the *"New York Times* of photographers' rights," meaning I wanted to take local stories from around the country and share them with a national audience while backing them up with a solid degree of credibility that would be built over time. The *New York Times*, after all, has been successfully branding itself for more than a century, doing it by earning more than 100 Pulitzer Prizes while touting their famous "All the News That's Fit to Print" motto.

It was only years later that I realized I had built a brand, reluctant as I initially was to incorporate a marketing buzzword into my journalistic goals. It was then that I decided to go full-forward and have a *Photography is Not a Crime* logo made, as well as

launch a merchandising line of products for sale (www.pinacnation.com).

After all, I'm not just a journalist, but an editor, a publisher, a marketer and a retailer (as well as an activist, public speaker and author).

And it's a brand that never stops evolving, never stops maturing; but it's also a brand that will always remain rooted to its original mission statement.

A perfect example of a journalistic brand evolving is *The New York Times* taking its original motto, which it started using on its masthead in 1897, and adjusting it to "All the News That's Fit to Click" in 2007 in a marketing campaign to promote its website.

As independent journalists, we don't have a fully staffed marketing department to promote our brand, so we must do it ourselves.

Photography is not a crime; It's a First Amendment right

HOME   ABOUT   PHOTOS   VIDEOS   CONTACT

JANUARY 2, 2008 - 1:06 AM

I'VE MOVED!!!

But only just down the street to wordpress.org where I bought a much larger blog with three columns instead of two.

Finally, I have some elbow room. This blog felt like too much like a Manhattan apartment. Plus, I never liked the idea of renting.

Now I have the ability to make my subhead grey and smaller than the headline, which gives it a much neater look. And the traffic in that area is not too bad.

Unfortunately, wordpress.com doesn't allow me to simply redirect this blog to that blog, so this blog has been getting a lot of visits lately, except I'm not around to play host.

Carlos Miller
- Carlos Miller
- Photography is not a crime

January 2009

APRIL 2007 TO DECEMBER 2008

Photography is Not a Crime
It's a First Amendment Right

HOME   ABOUT   PHOTOS   VIDEOS   FACEBOOK   CONTACT   RSS

PLEASE DONATE TO MY LEGAL DEFENSE FUND

Amount: $1.00
Website (Optional):
Donate

RECENT COMMENTS
- Real Estate Front—South Florida real estate blog on Did you vote for Barack Obama?
- Jake Stichler on Did you vote for Barack Obama?
- UNFAIR on What's the real story behind brash-talking Miami cop who pleaded guilty?
- eukager on Did you vote for Barack Obama?

← Photographers' rights in UK remain undefined as harassment continues
Kang Mango Strut Parade 2008 (video and photo cases) →

Amtrak photo contestant arrested by Amtrak police in NYC's Penn Station
December 27th, 2008 · 132 Comments

CAMERAS FOR EVERY BUDGET
B&H
To search, type and hit enter

MY SIDE OF THE STORY
My name is Carlos Miller and I am a multimedia journalist who was arrested by Miami police after taking photos of them against their wishes, a clear violation of my First Amendment rights. Since that arrest on Feb. 20th, 2007, I've been fighting a lengthy battle against the State of Florida in proving my innocence. Recently, a jury acquitted me of disobeying

JANUARY 2009 TO SEPTEMBER 2010

PINAC
PHOTOGRAPHY IS NOT A CRIME

pixiq
THE PHOTO WORLD IN FOCUS

▸ NEWS   ▸ GEAR   ▸ TECHNIQUES   ▸ CONTRIBUTORS   ▸ FOCUS   ▸ DISCOVER   search pixiq

Carlos Miller - Photography is Not a Crime   pixiq expert

Home ▸ Contributors ▸ Carlos Miller - Photography is Not a Crime

Posts from January 2012

Memphis Police Delete Photos From Journalist's Cell Phone Camera

The problem with the mainstream media is that too many reporters don't know the actual law when it comes to police confiscating cameras or deleting photos. And they think the only way to find out the law is to ask police. Take the recent case of Memphis police confiscating a cell phone from an ABC news photographer and deleting his photos after he snapped photos of them issuing a parking […]

About Me

Carlos Miller -...

Carlos Miller is a Miami multimedia journalist who has been arrested three times for recording cops in public.

He's beaten two of those cases, including a resisting arrest conviction that he had recently on View Profile »

Keep up with Carlos Miller - Photography is Not a Crime

Carlos Miller - Photography is Not a Crime on facebook »

SEPTEMBER 2010 TO OCTOBER 2012

PINAC
PHOTOGRAPHY IS NOT A CRIME

HOME • ABOUT • ADVERTISE • CONTACT • CONTRIBUTE • DONATE • MERCHANDISE • FORUMS   Search   SEARCH

Photography Is Not A Crime!
Like You like this.

PINAC NATION
PINAC Nation
Like You like this.

JANUARY 8TH, 2014

Federal Security Guard Assaults Man for Video Recording After Pointing Out Sign Allowing Video Recording 💬 2

BY CARLOS MILLER

Looking for information almost got me arrested

HELP SUPPORT PINAC

PINAC is mostly funded by its readers who contribute what they can to help pay for bandwidth costs, technical support, design adjustments and the countless hours I spend in front of the computer keeping it updated.

Donate

Proudly Sponsoring PINAC
Speedy and Reliable Hosting
NephoScale

OCTOBER 2012 TO PRESENT

HOME-MADE PRESS CREDENTIALS

ON NOVEMBER 24, 2010, MY BUDDY, TONY ANNESE, AND I ENTERED MIAMI INTERNATIONAL AIRPORT WITH OUR CAMERAS IN TOW TO PHOTOGRAPH AND RECORD THE TRANSPORTATION SECURITY ADMINISTRATION (TSA) CHECKPOINTS FOR THE STRAIGHTFORWARD PURPOSE OF SEEING HOW AUTHORITIES WOULD REACT.

It was the day before Thanksgiving, the busiest traveling day of the year, and the TSA checkpoints had come under much scrutiny and controversy because of its body scanners, which reveal intimate body parts, not to mention they've been alleged to cause cancer. I had written several articles on my blog about how TSA screeners forbid passengers to record the checkpoints when TSA policy allows the recording of checkpoints, an ongoing, annoying pattern of screeners refusing to abide by their own policies, which are clearly stated on their own website.

I was wearing a press pass that I had designed on Photoshop and had laminated at Staples, which displayed my name, photo and name of my company, Magic City Media, which is the limited liability company (LLC) under which *Photography is Not a Crime* falls (I've since had a new one designed specifically for PINAC but this was back when I was doing a lot more freelance journalistic work unrelated to my blog).

Tony wasn't wearing a press pass, which shouldn't have been a problem considering there is no law that gives credential-wearing journalists more legal rights than camera-wielding citizens with no credentials.

However, many cops are not trained in media law, so they are under the impression that credentials is what sets journalists apart from non-journalists.

And this became an issue that day, as you will see in the video by searching for "Testing the TSA policy on photographing checkpoints at Miami International Airport."

The first Miami-Dade police officer who approached us asked us not to record the checkpoints, but when we showed him the TSA printout that stated we were allowed to record the checkpoints, he took it over to other officials standing near the checkpoint before walking back, acknowledging that we had the right to record the checkpoints.

So we thanked him and walked off, satisfied that we were meeting our mission of educating authorities on the policy.

But when we started recording at a second checkpoint, another Miami-Dade police officer confronted us, asking us if we were "the press" and asking to see our "credentials." I showed her my home-made press pass, which she just glanced at, not even bothering to read my name, before honing in on Tony.

"You don't have the credentials, sir, that show you're the press. You can't be here... filming the checkpoint."

We informed her that she was misinformed and that all citizens, regardless of journalistic status, were allowed to record the checkpoints, but she wouldn't let it go, demanding Tony provide her with his driver's license.

A Miami-Dade police sergeant then arrived on the scene, who also insisted on asking Tony for his identification. Tony kept recording the checkpoint while asking them if they suspected him of committing a crime, which would be the only legal basis they would have to demand his identification.

WESTBORO BAPTIST CHURCH PROTEST, 2011

They informed him that they did not suspect him of committing a crime, but they still needed to see his identification. Tony respectfully stood his ground, which prompted them to have him walk towards the exit so they could call their lieutenant to clarify the law regarding the need to show identification if you record the checkpoint, if they had no reasonable suspicion he had committed a crime.

The whole episode lasted several minutes with the officers learning from their lieutenant that Tony was not under any legal obligation to provide identification if he wanted to record the checkpoints. So the officers didn't push the matter further and acknowledged they had been wrong, remaining respectful and cordial throughout the whole episode, even as they were insisting that Tony hand over his identification. And we ended up leaving the airport because we had already proved what we had set out to do; that we had the right to record the checkpoints. The interaction

with the cops could have been avoided had Tony worn press credentials, even if they were home-made, but it turned out for the better because we were able to educate the officers that recording the checkpoints was not just limited to the credentialed media, a term that has no legal bearing.

However, we also learned a lesson that day: If you want to do journalistic work without getting harassed or distracted by police, it makes sense to design your own press pass or hire a graphic designer to create one. But in doing so, it's important to use your real photo and name, and include the name of your company, your website address, your logo and your YouTube channel (if you have these), all to further establish your credentials. After all, we must remain as transparent and professional as possible in order to be treated as professionals.

The other advantage of wearing a press pass is that it can be used to identify yourself when a cop demands your identification as they tend to do when you are recording them on duty. As mentioned above, there is no legal requirement to produce an identification unless police have a reasonable suspicion that you have committed a crime. However, countless people have been arrested for refusing to provide identification, including Jeff Gray (see his profile on pages 34–37). These arrests never result in convictions, but that doesn't make up for the fact that they were placed in handcuffs and thrown in a dirty jail cell. As many cops will tell you, you can beat the rap, but you can't beat the ride.

GETTING ACCESS

Sometimes "home-made" can also mean simply "improvised." When I took photos of a bare-knuckle backyard boxing match in Miami in 2010 (pictured on the right), there wasn't exactly a formalized security process to go through and present authorized credentials to—far from it, the entire affair is very much underground and unofficial. Nevertheless, it wasn't as simple as walking right into the fight and snapping away. In these cases, having confidence and congeniality go a long way to gaining access to off-limits areas. Strike up a conversation, express your curiosity and interest in the subject, and ask permission to take photos. The receptiveness of most folks will surprise you.

BACKYARD BOXING, MIAMI, 2009

RISING TO THE OCCASION

LIKE MANY CITIZEN JOURNALISTS THAT HAVE EMERGED IN RECENT YEARS, PAUL WEISKEL DISCOVERED HIS PENCHANT FOR PHOTOJOURNALISM DURING THE OCCUPY WALL STREET PROTEST.

He was a 21-year-old political science major from the University of Massachusetts, Boston who had taken the bus to NYC after reading an ad calling for 20,000 people to "flood into lower Manhattan, set up tents, kitchens, peaceful barricades and occupy Wall Street for a few months." He didn't know what to expect but having watched the Arab Spring protests unfold in 2010 as well as having attended the Wisconsin State Capitol protests the following year during his spring break, he had a feeling it would be historic.

"I could sense a political tension in the country that would soon spill out onto the streets," he said. "I knew I wanted to be there to photograph it whenever it happened."

He was among the approximately 1,000 people that stormed Lower Manhattan and set up tents in Zuccotti Park on September 17, 2011, one of the many documenting the events with his camera. He posted hundreds of photos to Flickr (pweiskel08) during the first week, a time when the protest was mostly uneventful, receiving very little coverage from the mainstream media.

At first, the photos received very little attention because they didn't show much conflict, just protesters holding up signs and speaking through megaphones with a few bored cops looking on. But things got crazy on the seventh day when protesters clashed with police as they tried to march uptown during a demonstration.

"Up until then, things seemed to be predictable, but that day was much different," Weiskel said. "Police wanted to tighten their hold on their protests and the protesters wanted to do a longer and more visible march."

Police arrested more than 80 people that day and he came close to being arrested several times.

"Honestly, I think it's luck that I avoided arrest in my time photographing Occupy Wall Street, but I definitely got roughed up by the NYPD more than a few times."

During the chaos, he came across a group of protesters who had just been pepper sprayed by New York City Deputy Inspector Anthony Bologna—the cop credited with single-handedly escalating the protest when it became a global movement—as I chronicle in the Occupy Wall Street case study on pages 146-149.

"But I came up to the scene soon after the pepper spray was used so all I had to photograph was people having their eyes washed out," he said.

Later that day, he uploaded the photos to Flickr from his cousin's pad in Brooklyn and they immediately started going viral.

"I could follow the increased views on my phone and answer emails from people who had photo requests," he said. "I was a bit surprised and very pleased. But mostly I felt a sense of validation. I was doing hard work and I was putting a lot of time and energy into my photos in a very hostile environment."

CITIZEN PROFILE: PAUL WEISKEL

At the time, photography was just a hobby for Weiskel, so he set his photos with a creative commons copyright, which allowed other websites to use them as long as they credited him. So he was flattered when several of his photos were posted in *The Atlantic's* "In Focus" section on September 30, 2011, along with photos by professional photojournalists from the Associated Press, Getty, and Reuters.

Weiskel returned to school and began covering the Occupy Boston encampment where on April 15, 2012, he captured a powerful image of a Boston cop named Vaden Scantlebury grabbing a protester by the neck, which ended up published by *The Boston Globe*—again without compensation. Scantlebury then turned on him, attempting to block his shot, but Weiskel held his ground and kept snapping away. By now, thanks to his experience covering the Occupy Wall Street protests, he was seasoned to deal with such situations.

"I just wanted to stay calm and continue to try and take pictures," he said. "I wasn't surprised or intimated, I've had similar interactions with cops before so I didn't find it that shocking."

He then traveled back to New York City to cover the May Day protest—part of an international series of demonstrations and marches that take place annually on May 1 to protest against economic disparity—and ended up capturing another powerful image of a Black Bloc protester being manhandled by a Reuters photographer. That was when I came across his work as I have been ranting against the Black Bloc's habit of attacking photographers for years, writing about him on my blog on May 2, 2012. That Black Bloc protester also tried to knock Weiskel's camera out of his hand, but he wouldn't let him.

"I've been on both sides," he said. "I've been attacked by police for my photography and I've been attacked by protesters for my photography, but I'm not going to stop taking photos."

He has started charging publications for the use of his photos, which have appeared in *Mother Jones*, *Salon*, *The Huffington Post*, *Wired*, *PBS Newshour*, *Gawker*, *The Atlantic*, *The Progressive*, *Raw Story* and many more. But like many citizen journalists, he also depends on donations from his followers.

"Whether I get paid or not, I'm still going to be out there taking pictures," he said.

POLICE-ISSUED CREDENTIALS

IN THE 20TH CENTURY, IT WAS COMMON PROCEDURE FOR JOURNALISTS WHO COVER BREAKING NEWS TO OBTAIN CREDENTIALS THROUGH THEIR LOCAL POLICE DEPARTMENTS. BUT IT WAS MUCH EASIER TO DETERMINE WHO WAS A JOURNALIST BACK IN THOSE DAYS BECAUSE MOST WERE EITHER STAFFED BY NEWS ORGANIZATIONS OR FREELANCED FOR THEM.

After the rise in citizen journalism in the early 2000s, police departments started rethinking their policies on issuing press credentials with many doing away with the practice altogether. Back when I worked as a cop reporter for the San Bernardino Sun in the late 1990s, I had a press pass issued by the California Highway Patrol, which allowed me to cover murder scenes, house fires and traffic accidents without much hassle.

Occasionally, I would get escorted behind police lines to take a photo or catch a glimpse of a body, but I didn't have the right to cross police lines on a whim. And most of the time, they didn't have time to escort me behind lines until all the action died down anyway.

But the CHP terminated its program in 2004, saying it was getting swamped with requests from people that may or may not have been journalists, and that many people were abusing the press passes anyway by using them to get into baseball games and other events.

In the ensuing years, the Miami-Dade Police Department, the Boston Police

Department and the Orange County Sheriff's Office also terminated their programs.

Several lawsuits have emerged over the years from freelancers, student journalist and bloggers against police departments that still issue credentials on the basis that the practice is unconstitutional; essentially the government licensing journalists, which is not supposed to happen in a free country.

However, the New York City Police Department, the Metropolitan Police Department in Washington DC, the Los Angeles Police Department, the Los Angeles Sheriff's Department, the Seattle Police Department and the Chicago Police Department still maintain the practice, each of them with their own set of criteria on how to obtain them, which you can read on their respective websites.

During the Occupy Wall Street protests, NYPD cops were arresting journalists left and right, claiming they were doing so because they didn't have the police-issued credentials, even though they were also arresting fully credentialed professional reporters.

And several times during Occupy Wall Street, journalists wearing NYPD-issued credentials were restricted from entering public areas while allowing everybody else to walk through on the basis that if they started conducting mass arrests, the journalists would not be arrested.

Not only was this practice unconstitutional, it gave an edge to the citizen journalists who were able to document these arrests firsthand, even if a few of them were swept up in the arrests themselves.

So it doesn't hurt to apply for police-issued credentials, but it won't guarantee you any more legal rights than is already guaranteed by the First Amendment.

UNIV. OF MIAMI SIT-IN, 2007

SPECIAL-EVENT CREDENTIALS

MIAMI INTERNATIONAL WINE FAIR, 2010

ONE OF THE BIGGEST MISCONCEPTIONS I HAVE HEARD OVER THE YEARS IS THAT PRESS PASSES GUARANTEE YOU AUTOMATIC ENTRY INTO CONCERTS, SPORTING EVENTS AND OTHER SUCH FUN EVENTS. THE TRUTH IS, A PRESS PASS MAY MAKE IT EASIER FOR YOU TO OBTAIN MEDIA CREDENTIALS FOR THAT PARTICULAR EVENT, ALLOWING YOU FREE ENTRY AS WELL AS FREER ACCESS TO COVER THE EVENT.

But for the sake of all journalists, this is a privilege that should not be abused. And even then, a press pass is not necessarily a guarantee you will receive entry to a particular event. The rule of thumb is, the more prestigious the event, the harder it will be to obtain credentials. And it really helps if the event pertains to your niche of journalism, meaning if you're a food blogger, you will have a better chance of obtaining credentials for a food festival than if you run a blog on photographers' rights. Not that you shouldn't try, but if you really want to get in, do so with the intention it will be posted somewhere.

The key is to contact the public relations person before the event, preferably weeks, or even months if we're talking about an event like the Food Network South Beach Wine & Food Festival, which draws people from all over the world every February. It also helps if you're able to send them a letter with a letterhead containing your company logo, which is where branding comes in. But even if you decide at the last minute you want to cover the event, show up to the event and ask to speak to the public relations person in charge of distributing press passes.

Be sure to look the part. Bring your cameras, your business cards, your press pass and leave your family or significant other at home. You're there for a job, not a date. You also need to act like you belong there. Don't be rude, but don't be humble either. Just be professional. Tell them that you understand they are busy, which they will be, but that it's extremely important that you cover the event.

This is something I learned from my newspaper days when I had a major newspaper backing me, which I carried over to my blogging days, a confidence I saw lacking in other bloggers that never had the professional experience. They always seemed too shy to ask for the credentials or if they managed to talk to the person in charge, they would come across as if they were trying to get into a place where they didn't belong, so they naturally would be

denied. Act like you belong there and chances are, you will be granted the credentials. It's all about your attitude. After all, you must think of yourself as a professional in order for others to view you as a professional.

MONETIZING

NEW YORK, 2013

I WISH I HAD ENOUGH KNOWLEDGE ON MONETIZING JOURNALISM TO BE ABLE TO WRITE AN ENTIRE BOOK, RATHER THAN JUST A SINGLE SECTION, BUT THE REALITY IS, NOBODY IN THE BUSINESS SEEMS TO HAVE THE ANSWER ON MAKING A CONSISTENT PROFIT AT THE MOMENT.

Journalism is in a state of transition, with major news companies downsizing to the point of laying off entire photo staffs and independent journalists relying on donations and online ads that rarely cover hosting fees and camera gear, not to mention computers, travel expenses and even something as simple as a full tank of gas that enables them to drive to their assignments.

One problem is that online advertising doesn't bring in as much as print or television advertising, even if ironically the latter two are in a decline because readers and viewers are spending much more time online.

The other problem is that online publishers get a much smaller share of each ad sold compared to print publishers because Google takes a much larger cut from the initial ad sales compared to the commission ad salespeople receive from selling print ads.

And still another problem is that because online ads can be tracked, it is becoming evident that most readers just don't click on ads or block them altogether with software. This is why it's better to bypass Google AdSense for your blog, which only pays for click-through-rate (CTR), for an ad network that pays for cost per mille (CPM), meaning you get a fixed amount for each thousand impressions that people land on the web page containing the ad, regardless if they click on it or not.

You can also attempt to sell direct ads, but you will find that in order to do this successfully, you will need to dedicate just as much time to doing it as you do producing journalistic work.

There is money to be made on YouTube as we've read with Brian Bates (pages 68–71), who was able to quit his job and support himself and his wife with ad revenue generated through his prostitute-busting videos, and Joel Franco (pages 50–51), the high-school student who was making more than twice what his friends were making in their part-time jobs at fast food restaurants by making political-oriented videos.

But in order to consistently make money through online ads, whether it's through your blog or YouTube, you need to draw hundreds of thousands of page views every month, meaning you not only have to publish often, you need to publish content that can go viral.

This is why so many sites resort to link-baiting headlines, including Upworthy and BuzzFeed, where instead of writing headlines that are simple and direct as newspapers have done for centuries, they keep them vague but promising of some valuable insight, which usually ends up failing to meet the hype.

Or they resort to annoying pop-up ads or forcing you to click on ten pages to read an article that could have easily been published on a single web page.

It's not easy making money through online ads, so it's wise to seek other revenue streams to diversify.

I launched a merchandise line of *Photography is Not a Crime* T-shirts,

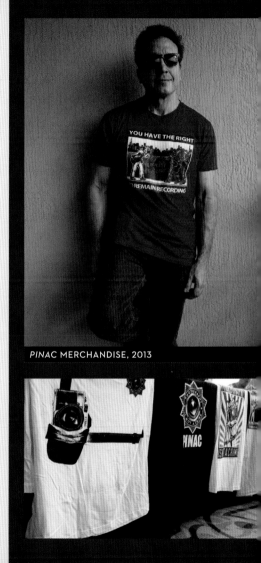

PINAC MERCHANDISE, 2013

caps, hoodies, stickers and patches that enabled me to further brand my site while bringing in a few extra dollars, which is something my friends over at *Cop Block* do as well. And we all depend on donations, but sometimes you have to remind your followers that their financial support is crucial to the work you do, but you don't want to overdo it either because that can turn them off.

Julie Dermansky, who is profiled on pages 78–81, has done an excellent job of making contacts at news sites where she regularly sells her articles, photos and videos, so she doesn't have to bother asking people for donations or frustrate herself with low ad revenue.

But she hustles just the same, never ceasing to pitch stories and find new clients, and her income is dependent on the economic stability of the news sites. The truth is, it's extremely difficult to make a liveable income as an independent journalist, so one option might be to team up with other like-minded citizen journalists where you can pool your resources and create a much more valuable product that will not only increase ad revenue but also attract donors.

PARADE, PARIS, 2013

The difficulty in monetizing journalism these days does not mean journalism is dying. On the contrary. Journalism is thriving more than it ever has with so many niches and options and voices, thanks to the internet. However, journalism has also been in a state of upheaval these last few years with the future of many newspapers uncertain and the implementation of a viable business model undiscovered.

Eventually the dust will settle and those who have built solid niches will be able to enjoy the fruits of their labor.

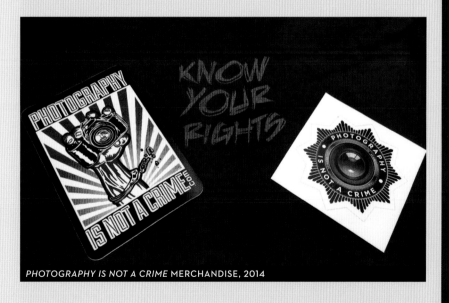

PHOTOGRAPHY IS NOT A CRIME MERCHANDISE, 2014

JOURNALISM ORGANIZATIONS

POLITICAL RALLY, PARIS, FRANCE, 2012

LIKE MANY OCCUPATIONS, JOURNALISM HAS ITS SHARE OF PROFESSIONAL ORGANIZATIONS THAT WILL HELP YOU PROSPER IN YOUR NEWLY FOUND CAREER. THE BENEFITS CAN INCLUDE NETWORKING, EDUCATION, AND EVEN LEGAL SUPPORT IF YOU EVER NEED IT. FOR DECADES, THESE ORGANIZATIONS CONSISTED MOSTLY OF FULL-TIME PROFESSIONALS, JOURNALISM PROFESSORS AND STUDENTS AND INTERNS HOPING TO BECOME FULL-TIME PROFESSIONALS.

But these days, many of the older organizations have adjusted with the times and have begun accepting citizen journalists as members. However, newer organizations have emerged dedicated to the citizen journalist.

There are way too many organizations to post here, including many that have faded away as quickly as they emerged, and others dedicated to diversity in the newsrooms, which probably doesn't do us any good considering we make our newsrooms wherever we set up our computers.

For a full list, check out www. journalismassociations.com/members/.

The following are organizations that I believe would be helpful to the citizen journalist:

National Press Photographers Association
www.nppa.org

Over the years, NPPA general counsel Mickey Osterreicher has written countless letters to police chiefs whose officers have arrested citizens for recording, offering to train their officers in the law. Many times, these citizens are not even members of the NPPA. But they provide much, much more to visual journalists.

Society of Professional Journalists
www.spj.org

SPJ was the first organization that reached out to me after my first arrest, even though I wasn't a member, contributing to my legal defense fund and writing letters of protest to the local police chief and mayor. I've seen them defend numerous citizen journalists over the years going through the same fate.

Investigative Reporters and Editors
www.ire.org

I spent many years as a member of IRE during my newspaper years and they provide a wealth of educational resources that show you how to break stories that otherwise would not get published.

Online News Association
www.journalists.org

At a time when membership in most journalism organizations were declining due to the economic downturn that has affected newsrooms throughout the country, the ONA was the only organization that saw an increase in membership.

Digital Media Law Project
www.dmlp.org

Formerly called the Citizen Media Law Project, the DMLP is not an organization you join by paying dues, but it is a website you should become very familiar with because it provides extensive legal tips, guidelines and a state-by-state breakdown of laws that might affect journalists. Also, I've met and spoken to directors Jeff Hermes and Andy Sellars on several occasions and they have proven to be extremely helpful in providing general legal advice free of charge.

WATCHING THE WATCHMEN

JACOB CRAWFORD ARRIVED IN OAKLAND IN 2000 AT THE AGE OF 21, HOPING TO BE A FILMMAKER, BUT NOT EXACTLY SURE WHAT HE WANTED TO FOCUS ON. THAT QUICKLY CHANGED WHEN HE SAW THE HEAVY-HANDEDNESS OF THE OAKLAND POLICE DEPARTMENT ON POOR MINORITIES, ESPECIALLY BLACKS.

"For the first time in my life, I was watching the status quo of police pulling people over for not being white," he said. "It was just so routine and common. As a white guy, I had never seen anything like that before."

He would later learn that relations between the city's police department and its black residents have been tense since the end of World War II, when the police department began recruiting white southerners to police the growing influx of black residents. Tensions continued to mount during the turbulent 1960s with the rise of the Black Panther Party, founded in Oakland as a response to the police abuse in black neighborhoods. The situation became even worse in 1968 after Oakland police killed Black Panther Bobby Hutton by shooting him more than 12 times, even though he had stripped down to his underwear to prove he was unarmed as he tried to surrender after a shootout. By the time Crawford arrived in Oakland, the city was reeling from yet another police abuse scandal involving a group of rogue officers known as "the Riders."

"They were kidnapping people, torturing them, planting evidence, beating people up," he said.

So he decided to try and make a difference with his camera, hoping to catch some of these cops in an illegal act. The first thing he did was reach out to Copwatch, the first organized group that used cameras to hold police accountable (and discussed in detail on pages 138–141). Copwatch has since expanded in cities throughout the United States, mostly in the west, predating organizations like Cop Block and Peaceful Streets, and, of course, my blog, *Photography is Not a Crime*. He spoke to one of their lawyers, learning that it was not illegal to videotape police in public. However, they warned him that it could be dangerous because police do not appreciate being videotaped. But he decided to do it anyway, at first, trying his best to remain discreet, videotaping from behind bushes and buildings. Then he gathered some friends and started getting braver, and more open about videotaping, which was not easy at first.

"My first few times were horrifying," he said.

It got to the point where police began trying to intimidate him.

"I had an incident with a cop where he told me I was going to get shot," he said. "He told me he knew who I was, knew what I did, and that he had his eye on me."

So he became a member of Berkeley Copwatch, learning from them how best to video record cops while avoiding direct confrontation.

"You need to treat them like wild animals," he said. "You walk up to them slowly, not making eye contact."

"You don't want to startle them. They're dangerous like that."

CITIZEN PROFILE: JACOB CRAWFORD

Crawford quickly demonstrated a talent for video editing, putting footage together to create compelling storylines complete with professional cuts and background music. In 2003, he released a 50-minute documentary for Copwatch titled *These Streets are Watching*, an educational film about using cameras to hold police accountable. But YouTube would not be launched until two years later, so the film was mainly distributed through DVDs, making it harder for people to stumble upon it as so many do these days with these types of videos. It has since been uploaded to YouTube, so it's a recommended watch, just to get a grasp on how citizen journalism evolved with groups like Copwatch as well as to appreciate Crawford's video-editing skills.

Crawford also developed a knack for investigative journalism over the years, which he uses to expose police abuse and policy violations. These skills came to light during the 2011 Occupy Oakland protests in which he exposed that officers were not turning on their body-mounted cameras as they moved in to disperse protesters, sometimes quite violently.

"They got in trouble for that, they got disciplined because they broke policy," he said.

Crawford, along with *East Bay Express* journalist Ali Winston, reviewed countless clips of video footage to determine the identity of a police officer who had tossed a flash-bang grenade into a crowd of protesters after they had rushed in to help an Iraq War veteran, who had just suffered a cracked skull from a bean bag projectile fired by another police officer. Check out the video by searching for "Oakland policeman throws flash grenade into crowd trying to help injured protester." They discovered that the officer, Robert Roche, had killed three people in the line of duty since 2006, cleared of all of them, even though the families of one of the victims received a $500,000 wrongful death settlement.

By 2012, Crawford's reputation was renowned in the Bay Area, so he was contacted by the National Lawyer's Guild, which hired him to review countless clips of police and citizen

video to recreate scenes from the Occupy Oakland protests where police once again demonstrated heavy-handed tactics. His work helped the guild secure a $1.17 million settlement for 12 plaintiffs that were injured by police.

"I just want the police to know that I'm not afraid of them and I'm not afraid to record them and I'm not afraid to expose them," he said.

MEDIA LAW

PROTEST OUTSIDE NEW YORK LIBRARY, NYC, 2011

AFTER DELIBERATING FOR MORE THAN TWO HOURS, THE JURY EMERGED FROM THEIR CHAMBERS AND HANDED THE BAILIFF THEIR VERDICT, FINDING ME NOT GUILTY ON ALL COUNTS EXCEPT RESISTING ARREST WITHOUT VIOLENCE.

The judge, who took a huge disliking to me, slapped me with one year of probation, 50 hours of community service, and eight hours of an anger-management class—even though the Miami police officers were the ones so enraged that they couldn't resist bashing my forehead into the sidewalk as they arrested me for taking photos

Not only did he give me a much harsher sentence than sought by the prosecutor, Judge Jorge Fernandez then laid into me about my blogging, before stating, "I'm shocked at your lack of remorse."

But I wasn't going to show remorse for taking photos of cops. And the only reason the jury convicted me was

the witness stand, which allowed the state to enter my blog as evidence, even though I did not launch it until two months after my 2007 arrest.

When the prosecutor kept hammering away about a blog post where I compared a group of Los Angeles police officers to Nazis because they had been caught on camera bashing kids and reporters with batons, I became defensive, combative and sarcastic, which gave the wrong impression to the jury.

So even though they determined I was innocent of disobeying a lawful order and disorderly conduct, they assumed that I would resist arrest, which is absurd considering they had determined the initial arrest to be unlawful. But that's Florida justice for you.

In hindsight, the guilty verdict turned out to be a blessing in disguise because otherwise, I would have shut the blog down and moved on with my life, having proved that photography is not a crime. But the guilty verdict left me with something more to prove; that I did not receive a fair trial. So after discovering that appellate lawyers would charge $10,000 to take the case, I decided to appeal it *pro se*, which is legal jargon for representing myself.

I then spent the next several weeks in the University of Miami law library, reading up on case law and preparing an appeal that would eventually get the conviction reversed, with the help of my attorney and friend, Michael Pancier, who coached me along the way.

It was one of the proudest moments of my life, considering I'd never set foot in a law class. You can read the appellate decision along with my arguments and prosecutor's rebuttal by searching for "Carlos Miller's appeal victory."

The beauty of the law is that it's written in black and white and available in law libraries across the United States, if not at your fingertips through the internet, accessible to anybody without a law license. A great site for citizen journalists is the Digital Media Law Project (**www.dmlp.org**).

So it's in your best interest to learn the law because you just never know when you will have to defend yourself.

FTAA PROTESTS, MIAMI, 2003

COMMERCIAL VS. EDITORIAL USE

GAY RIGHTS RALLY, MIAMI, 2011

ALTHOUGH THE DIFFERENCES BETWEEN EDITORIAL AND COMMERCIAL PHOTOGRAPHY ARE PRETTY EASY TO UNDERSTAND, THERE ARE MANY PEOPLE WHO NEVER FAIL TO CONFUSE THE TWO, BELIEVING THAT IF YOU ARE SHOOTING FOR A BLOG THAT CONTAINS ADS, THEN YOU ARE SHOOTING COMMERCIAL, AND THEREFORE, REQUIRED TO OBTAIN MODEL RELEASE FORMS FROM YOUR SUBJECTS AS WELL AS FACE RESTRICTIONS FROM SHOOTING IN CERTAIN PUBLIC AREAS.

If that were the case, then photojournalists throughout history would have been severely restricted from doing their job because newspapers and news stations both operate on ad revenue.

Commercial photography would be if you're actually shooting one of those ads. These include the models in the glossy magazines or the high-end cars you see advertised or anything for that matter, including the well-dressed couple clinking glasses of champagne by the pool, advertising, of course, the champagne. If you're reading this book, odds are that you're not interested in commercial photography, although it pays a lot more than photojournalism (but see pages 98–101).

Quite simply, editorial photography is photojournalism. It is the photos you see in the articles that appear next to the ads. It is determined, but not limited, by the newsworthiness of a photo. It can also be used for educational purposes like textbooks.

But it must be an accurate portrayal of a subject whether it is a protester waving a flag, a cop making an arrest or a politician giving a speech.

Editorial photography captures reality and presents it as such.

Commercial photography, in most cases, creates a scene that looks like reality in order to sell a product or promote a service.

Or it could use an editorial photo in order to sell a product or promote a service; perhaps a lawyer using the photo of an arrest to promote his business, ensuring clients that he would fight for their rights if they are unlawfully arrested.

In other words, you can take an editorial photograph for a news site, then turn it into a commercial photograph if a potential client approaches you and asks for permission to use your image in an advertisement. However, in this case, you must then be able to obtain a model release. If you allow the client to use the photo in the ad without a model release, then that model can sue you—easily.

If you shoot enough editorial photographs, you will probably be threatened with lawsuits by people who are clueless about the laws. But as long as you know the differences, you have nothing to worry about.

STREET SMARTS

If you haven't yet had someone yell at you to "get that camera out of my face," consider yourself lucky. Some people are just instantly suspicious of cameras and eager to pick a fight with a photographer doing his job. It comes with the territory. The best advice in such situations is to keep your cool, and without escalating the situation, state that you're a photographer and you have the legal right to take photos in public spaces. In such cases, a simple business card can come in very handy (to say nothing of some credentials—see pages 86–89). A lot of this can be preempted by smiling just and acting professionally when you're on a shoot.

PUBLIC VS. PRIVATE PROPERTY

THE FIRST AMENDMENT PRETTY MUCH GUARANTEES US THE RIGHT TO PHOTOGRAPH ANYTHING WE CAN SEE FROM PUBLIC PROPERTY, INCLUDING POLICE, PARAMEDICS, VICTIMS, SUSPECTS, GOVERNMENT BUILDINGS, INFRASTRUCTURES, PRIVATE BUSINESSES AND EVEN PRIVATE RESIDENTS. THE GENERAL RULE IS, IF YOU CAN SEE IT WHILE STANDING IN PUBLIC, YOU CAN PHOTOGRAPH OR VIDEO RECORD IT.

However, this doesn't mean you won't face arrest, even if you are not breaking the law. Cops will threaten to arrest you for everything from interference and obstruction to loitering and resisting arrest, depending on what state you live in. Or if you are video recording paramedics tending to a victim, they will accuse you of violating the The Health Insurance Portability and Accountability Act of 1996 (HIPAA), which has to do with internal medical records, not patients being treated in public.

The key to documenting news in public is to not break any obvious law that they can nail you for, such as standing in the street or getting too close to and interfering with the investigation. If other people are allowed to stand around and watch, then you are allowed to video record. And no matter what they say, police cannot seize your footage as evidence without a subpoena, unless there happens to be exigent circumstances, meaning they have a strong suspicion you will destroy the footage.

However, the rules are a little different on private property that is open to the public such as a business establishment where you are subjected to rules by the owner, even if nobody has an expectation of privacy there either. But even the owners of the property don't have the right to confiscate your camera or order you to delete your footage if they catch you recording. The most they can do is order you to leave the premises and have you arrested for trespassing if you refuse to leave.

So if you find yourself in a situation where, say, a fight breaks out in a shopping mall, don't be afraid to start recording because not only will you be capturing compelling footage, your footage may help investigators determine who should be charged in case somebody gets seriously injured. Not that you should hand over your footage to the police if they ask for it. If anything, give them a copy of your footage or hand them your business card, so they know where to look when it goes online. If you allow them to make a copy, you still have the right to publish

that footage, even if police try to tell you otherwise.

I don't suggest becoming enemies with the police, but I highly recommend against allowing them to dictate what you can and cannot publish. As an independent journalist, it is important to remain as independent as possible because any perceived relationship with the police may hinder you in future stories with non-police sources.

ELEVENTH ANNIVERSARY OF SEPTEMBER 11TH, NEW YORK CITY, 2012

KEEPING THEM HONEST

IN AND OUT OF PRISON FOR MORE THAN TWO DECADES, AL CRESPO IS HARDLY THE PERSON YOU'D EXPECT TO BE HOLDING THE GOVERNMENT TO ACCOUNT.

The septuagenarian hasn't robbed a bank since the 1970s. He was last released from prison in 1984, and is now a reformed-robber-turned-rabble-rouser, doing what the local media has refused to do by exposing the never-ending shenanigans and corruption in Miami.

"How f***ed-up do you think this county is when people are turning to a bank robber, ex-convict for salvation," Crespo asked from his Miami home.

Somebody has to do the job considering the *Miami Herald* is but a fragment of its former self, a paper that once reigned in the state in circulation and Pulitzer Prizes, but dropped to fifth in circulation before it was forced to relocate to the western suburbs of the county after The McClatchy Company sold the landmark waterfront property to a Malaysian casino company.

"The tips I get come from insiders who tipped off the *Miami Herald* or the *Miami New Times*, but they sit on the stories, so they turn to me and I put them up the next day."

Many times, the local media is forced to follow up on the stories he breaks

on his blog, the *Crespogram Report* (www.crespogram.com). But most of the time, they just pretend it never happened.

Crespo, who spent a dozen years traveling the country photographing protests for a long-term project on activism that resulted in a book called *Protest in the Land of Plenty*, acknowledges he doesn't receive a ton of page views because he is not as social media savvy as other citizen journalists, stubbornly refusing to use Facebook to spread his content. But the people who do read his blog are the movers and shakers of Miami-Dade County; the mayors, the commissioners, the police chiefs, the cops, and all those tax-funded public officials working for the various departments, including those that tip him off and those that get exposed.

Crespo launched the blog in April 2010 for the sole purpose of exposing an act of cronyism by the newly elected mayor of Miami, Tomás Regalado, who hired his buddy, Harry Emilio Gottlieb, to head the city's Film and Cultural Affairs Department after taking office in January. Crespo, who became a film location scout after he was released from prison, realized the mayor's new hire was proving to be detrimental to the county's multimillion dollar film industry. So he kept hammering away at the issue on his blog until Gottlieb was fired by December of that year.

FTAA PROTESTS, MIAMI, 2003

CITIZEN PROFILE: AL CRESPO

Then he received a tip about Miami City Commissioner Marc Sarnoff illegally operating a fully staffed law firm from one of his houses in Coconut Grove, which was a fairly blatant city code violation. Code enforcers began citing him, only for Sarnoff to use his clout to get the citations dismissed. So Crespo kept hammering away, posting photo evidence that the commissioner was in clear violation of the city code, before Sarnoff was finally pressured to move his law office to downtown Miami.

"Nobody knew who I was at that time, so I would hand out my cards at city hall, telling people to check out my site," Crespo said.

Crespo said he was pretty clueless as to how the local governments operated before launching his blog, but he quickly learned. And he quickly developed a reputation for publishing factual stories that were backed up by public records. However, his inexperience with technology also drove him to launch the blog on iWeb, a easy-to-use platform that came with

several limitations and has since been discontinued by Apple. He also stubbornly refuses to use Facebook to further promote his blog, a platform all citizen journalists should be using. But at his age, he said he couldn't be bothered to learn more than he must, satisfied that the right people are reading his blog, content that his blog has made a difference. In fact, the *Miami New Times* named him Miami's top blogger in 2012, stating that "despite his brazen, notorious past—or perhaps because of it—Crespo has become a leader in confronting Miami's most powerful politicians and public officials."

In June 2011, Crespo reported that Mayor Regalado had tried to "bribe" Miami Police Chief Miguel Exposito with $400,000 to step down after a long-running feud over electronic slot machines that were popular in cafeterias, markets and laundromats throughout the county. The mayor, who had received $14,000 in campaign contributions from the company that built the machines, defended them, claiming they were no different than video games—strictly for amusement. However, Exposito believed they were illegal gambling machines, so he had officers raid the businesses that had them, confiscating more than 100 machines that were determined to be rigged, according to a casino expert from Atlantic City. The mayor denied everything to the local media, who were following up on Crespo's story.

But then Exposito called a press conference confirming it was true, further cementing Crespo's reputation for getting the facts straight. Exposito was eventually fired and Crespo moved on to other stories about the Miami Police Department, including one where he revealed that police had planted a gun on a drug suspect they had arrested to beef up the charges.

"The cops tipped me off on that one," he said. "They gave me an audio tape and transcripts that proved they falsified a report."

117

COPYRIGHT VIOLATIONS VS. FAIR USE

THE 2010 HAITIAN EARTHQUAKE CAME WITHOUT WARNING, THE WAY THEY ALWAYS DO, BUT THIS ONE SHOOK HARDER, LONGER AND LOUDER THAN MOST, KILLING AN ESTIMATED 100,000 PEOPLE BY THE TIME THE AFTERSHOCKS HAD SUBSIDED.

Independent photojournalist and native Haitian Daniel Morel, 59, was just leaving a friend's house when the earthquake struck on January 12. As he explains in an interview with *Time* (which I encourage you to listen to by searching Google for the story "The First Photographs from Port-au-Prince of the Haiti Earthquake"):

"It was very frightening because of the noise," he said in the audio interview, which includes sounds of the earthquake along with his photos. "I've never heard noise like that. [...] The earth was going like a wave."

When the earth stopped shaking, he began taking photos, focusing on a woman who was being rescued beneath a pile of rubble, her black face covered in white dust, augmenting her shocked expression.

In less than an hour, with the help of a friend, Morel uploaded thirteen photos to a newly created TwitPic account, a social media platform that allows users to upload photos that can be posed on Twitter, making it very useful for citizen journalists. Although he stated that his photos were available for purchase, the photos were immediately downloaded by a Dominican man named LIsandro Suero, who re-uploaded them to his own TwitPic account claiming they were his, quickly selling them to the French newswire service, Agence France-Presse (AFB), who in turn passed them to American stock photo agency Getty under an existing agreement. Getty, in turn, began selling the photos to newspapers throughout the world.

By the following day, Morel's photos were printed in newspapers everywhere, but with Suero's byline, who wasn't even a photojournalist. Morel, who had been a photojournalist for 25 years (including a stint with the Associated Press) engaged an attorney, who began sending out cease-and-desist letters. This prompted several organizations, including the *Wall Street Journal*, NBC, and the Associated Press, to pay Morel for the use of the photos and give him proper credit. But AFP and Getty responded by suing Morel, as incredible as that sounds, claiming he was making an "antagonistic assertion of rights" by demanding payment for his own photos. They also claimed that once the photos were on Twitter, they were in the "public domain," and therefore, available for the taking.

Morel's lawyers countersued and thus began a three-year battle that resulted in AFP and Getty paying Morel $1.2 million, a huge victory for photographers and citizen journalists, but also a wake-up call to bloggers who routinely use news photos under the "fair use" argument. But what if Morel did not have 25 years of professional experience where he expected payment for his work?

CHILDREN IN CITE SOLEIL, HAITI, 2003

Minutes after US Airways Flight 1549 departed from La Guardia Airport in New York City on January 15, 2009, it flew into a flock of geese, causing its engines to malfunction and forcing the pilot to land the plane in the Hudson River. Watching the scene unfold from a ferry, Jānis Krūms pulled out his smartphone and snapped a photo, uploading it to TwitPic before posting it on Twitter.

The photo ended up getting retweeted hundreds of times, winding up on the home pages of several news sites from around the world. And for the next several days, Krūms was the man of the hour, being interviewed by endless news stations, all of them celebrating citizen journalism scoop. Yet none of them offered him any payment. And being completely unprepared for the situation, he didn't bother asking for compensation. Essentially, the media had the same approach to Krūms' photo as it did to Morel's photo, treating it as if it were in the public domain. But what exactly is "the public domain?"

"The public domain is not a place but rather a legal term pertaining to a work that is no longer under copyright protection," said Mickey Osterreicher, general counsel for the National Press Photographers Association.

"While works in the public domain may be used freely without the permission of the former copyright owner, far too many users believe that if a photograph is posted on the internet, it is there for their use without permission, credit or compensation and any such use is 'fair.'"

You will hear many bloggers refer to the fair use argument when lifting content to place on their site, and I've used that excuse myself, not that I have ever been called on it. I justify it by allowing use of my photos on other blogs when they are referring to one of my stories. But I've had lawyers send out cease-and-desist letters when sites have lifted my entire articles as if I had written them solely for them.

My personal rule is to allow sites to lift a few paragraphs before linking to my

THE U.S. LAW

UNDER THE U.S. COPYRIGHT LAW, FOUR CRITERIAS MUST BE TAKEN INTO CONSIDERATION BEFORE A PARTICULAR WORK CAN BE CONSIDERED FAIR USE, WHICH ALLOWS COPYRIGHTED WORK TO BE REPUBLISHED WITHOUT PERMISSION FROM ITS OWNER.

1. THE PURPOSE AND CHARACTER OF THE USE, INCLUDING WHETHER SUCH USE IS OF COMMERCIAL NATURE OR IS FOR NON-PROFIT EDUCATIONAL PURPOSES

2. THE NATURE OF THE COPYRIGHTED WORK

3. THE AMOUNT AND SUBSTANTIALITY OF THE PORTION USED IN RELATION TO THE COPYRIGHTED WORK AS A WHOLE

4. THE EFFECT OF THE USE UPON THE POTENTIAL MARKET FOR, OR VALUE OF, THE COPYRIGHTED WORK

site, a habit I abide by when using content from other sites. The truth is, there are no established parameters as to what defines fair use because rarely does anybody spend the time, money and energy to take the issue to court. But as we saw with Morel, the courts will most likely side with the copyright owner, which is not a bad thing.

The key is to be prepared to ask for compensation when posting a photo that gets picked up by a news site or agency. And to be prepared for a legal battle if they respond with the arrogance that they did to Morel. Ultimately, you must recognize the value of your content.

TOUR DE FRANCE, PARIS, 2013

WIRETAPPING

REPUBLICAN NATIONAL CONVENTION, 2012

IN 2006, POLICE IN NEW HAMPSHIRE BANGED ON MICHAEL GANNON'S DOOR, DEMANDING TO TALK TO HIS TEENAGE SON WHO WAS SUSPECTED OF COMMITTING A MUGGING IN DOWNTOWN NASHUA. GANNON TOLD THE OFFICERS TO GO AWAY, BUT HE SAID THEY RESPONDED BY POINTING A SHOTGUN AT HIS HEAD AND BARGING INSIDE, NOT FINDING HIS SON.

Gannon captured the incident on his home surveillance video system, so he took the footage down to the Nashua Police Department to file a complaint against the officers. But he ended up being arrested on felony wiretapping charges, facing 21 years in prison.

The following year, police in Pennsylvania pulled over a pair of teens for speeding, but ended up arresting passenger Brian Kelly on felony wiretapping charges because he was video recording the stop from the passenger seat. Kelly, 18, spent 26

hours in jail following the arrest, and faced a possible seven years in prison.

Then there was Simon Glik, a Massachusetts lawyer who came across a group of Boston police officers making an arrest in a public park on October 1, 2007. Believing they were being abusive, he pulled out his cell phone and began video recording, only to be arrested on, you guessed it, felony wiretapping charges. Charges against all three men were dismissed but those arrests sparked a nationwide trend within police departments throughout

UNIVERSITY OF MIAMI SIT-IN, 2007

the country to begin twisting their state's wiretapping laws to arrest citizen journalists.

The national mainstream media finally caught wind of the absurdity in 2010 after Maryland State Police arrested Anthony Graber, a 25-year-old National Guardsman, for uploading a video he recorded on a helmet cam showing a plainclothes police officer pulling him over at gunpoint for speeding on his motorcycle. By then, it became clear that police were using these laws to intimidate citizens from holding them

accountable when the laws were originally designed to protect the privacy of telephone conversations.

The intimidation became even more evident in 2010 when an overzealous prosecutor from Illinois named Anita Alvarez prosecuted a woman for recording a conversation with internal affairs officers as they tried to intimidate her from filing a complaint against another officer who had groped her breast during a domestic abuse investigation.

So how can you protect yourself as a citizen journalist from an unsuspecting felony charge that can land you in prison with hardened criminals? For starters, it is best to get in the habit of receiving consent before you begin audio recording a telephone interview, even if you are in a one-party consent state, because you don't want to unintentionally break the law by calling somebody in another state and forgetting to receive consent. This can be done simply by informing them you are recording from the beginning of the conversation or if you want to be extra careful, ask for their consent before you start recording, then ask them to confirm their consent once you are recording.

It's best to get in the habit of openly and blatantly recording video when you are out in public (even though Massachusetts is the only state that explicitly makes it a crime to secretly record people in public) because you want to remain as transparent as possible, and you don't want to have a judge or jury determine what constitutes an expectation of privacy.

Most states, as well as Washington D.C., are one-party consent states, meaning that as long as one person in the conversation consents to the recording, then they are legally allowed to audio record it without the other person's permission or knowledge. However, 12 states—California, Connecticut, Florida, Illinois, Hawaii, Maryland, Massachusetts, Montana, Nevada, New Hampshire, Pennsylvania and Washington—all-party consent states, according to the Digital Media

Law Project, a site every citizen journalist should become familiar with (www.dmlp. org). All but one of these states include an expectation of privacy provision, meaning if you record a conversation with a person in an area where they would have no expectation of privacy, which is where most interactions with police take place, then the laws would not apply.

But Illinois has no such provision, making it the most Draconian wiretapping law in the country. That is, before a federal judge issued a permanent injunction in April 2013, preventing it from ever being prosecuted in Cook County again. This ended a two-year battle between the ACLU and State Attorney Anita Alvarez, who seemed hell-bent on jailing anybody who dared record a police officer in public without their consent. Six months earlier, the U.S. Supreme Court had refused to hear the case on Alvarez's request after the Seventh U.S. Circuit Court of Appeals determined the law to be unconstitutional, upholding that ruling. This, however,

wouldn't stop police in other Illinois counties to arrest citizens, but it would make it much harder to prosecute them, much less convict them.

The Massachusetts wiretapping law has also proven to be dangerous because it makes it a crime to secretly record others, including police officers, even if they are in public and do not have an expectation of privacy, which has led to the arrest and conviction of several people, including a citizen journalist named Jeffrey Manzelli, who was arrested in 2002 after interviewing cops with a microphone in his hand, simply because he did not verbally tell them he was recording.

But Simon Glik, the attorney arrested in 2007 for video recording Boston police making an arrest, decided to fight back after his charges were dropped. He filed a lawsuit, but police moved to dismiss it on the basis of qualified immunity. The motion was denied, prompting them to appeal to the First Circuit Court of Appeals. In August 2011, the First Circuit Court of Appeals came down with a landmark ruling that was monumental for citizen journalists, stating that citizens have the same rights to record public officials in public as members of the media, which was one reason why the U.S. Supreme Court refused to hear the Illinois case in November 2012:

The proliferation of electronic devices with video-recording capability means that many of our images of current events come from bystanders with a ready cell phone or digital camera rather than a traditional film crew, and news stories are now just as likely to be broken by a blogger at her computer as a reporter at a major newspaper. Such developments make clear why the news-gathering protections of the First Amendment cannot turn on professional credentials or status.

INTERNATIONAL LAW

Throughout this chapter, I've been describing United States media law. If you find yourself interacting with or doing work in other nations, it's absolutely imperative to familiarize yourself with the relevant legal jargon. For instance, privacy laws in France are considerably stricter than in the U.S., and the United Kingdom has laws against libel and slander that often catch foreigners by surprise. Similarly, not all copyright protection is created equally—though there are ongoing efforts to create international standards under the Berne Convention. Simply put, if you're working in another country, err on the side of caution, and do some thorough research on the relevant law.

PALESTINIAN RALLY, MIAMI, 2008

CITIZEN JOURNALISM IS ACTIVISM

MAJOR NANCY PEREZ, MIAMI, 2012

AFTER ALMOST FIVE YEARS OF RUNNING MY BLOG, I HAD BECOME NOTORIOUS AMONG THE LOCAL POLICE DEPARTMENTS FOR KEEPING A RUNNING TAB ON COPS WHO ARREST CITIZENS WITH CAMERAS. THAT'S NOT TO MENTION THE FACT THAT I HAD BEEN ARRESTED TWICE FOR TAKING PICTURES OF COPS DURING JOURNALISTIC ASSIGNMENTS WITHOUT A SINGLE CONVICTION.

So I should not have been surprised when I was arrested a third time on January 31, 2012 while covering the Occupy Miami eviction from county hall, which was one of many encampments taking place throughout the country, inspired by Occupy Wall Street. I was shooting only stills during my first two arrests, but I was video recording the third time around, so I captured a much more comprehensive record of this arrest. But when I was released from jail the following day and had retrieved my cameras, I realized they had deleted the last clip in the hard drive, which is illegal but happens quite often because there are very little repercussions. However, I was able to recover the footage using free software that I downloaded from the internet called Photo Rec, which enabled me to post it on YouTube and on my blog, where it quickly went viral with the help of *The Huffington Post, Ars Technica,* and *Boing Boing,* just to name a few. The video shows Miami-Dade Police Major Nancy Perez confronting me as I was walking down a sidewalk during the moments after they had evicted all the activists. The video also shows several other journalists, including veteran *Miami Herald* reporter Glenn Garvin, as well as a few television videographers.

I was told I was being arrested because I did not disperse with the rest of the activists. I did not disperse with them because I was never part of them. I covered the Occupy Miami movement and I was sympathetic towards their cause, but I was also critical of it. And the only time I ever camped out at county hall was as a journalist because I wrote a series of articles on it for a local website. But Perez, who was the department's media spokesperson, said she had no idea who I was, so she assumed I was an activist. And it really didn't make a difference considering one doesn't have more legal rights than the other.

We later found out the department's Homeland Security Bureau had been monitoring my Facebook page and had sent out my photo to all the commanding officers earlier that day, including Perez, informing them I would be covering the eviction. So Perez knew exactly who I was when she ordered a group of cops to arrest me. Despite the video evidence that I had been singled out from the other journalists, the Miami-Dade State Attorney's Office insisted on going through with the case as it has always done with my arrests.

MIAMI DADE COURTHOUSE, 2012

OWS MIAMI PROTEST, 2012

MAJOR NANCY PEREZ, 2012

PROSECUTOR ARI PREGEN, 2012

Florida allows cameras in courtrooms, so I brought in my friend, Bruce Stanley, who was part of the Occupy Miami movement, to video record the trial (I'd I've known him from years earlier). And not surprisingly, the prosecution tried to convince the jury that I was not a journalist, but rather an activist. But as my attorney Arnold Trevilla (who was defending me for the third time in five years) pointed out, I was only an activist in their eyes because I stand up for my rights as a journalist.

Prosecutors said the reason the other journalists were not arrested was because they had remained behind police lines during the evacuation, meaning the media was essentially embedded with the police department, making it hardly objective. As an independent journalist, I remained in front of the police lines as my goal was to ensure they did not use excessive force against the protesters as was happening during other Occupy evictions throughout the country. I was also not afraid to challenge them when

they used their riot shields to try and block me from video recording an arrest. This angered Perez because she testified that I had called her "some names" during that exchange, which was not true. Minutes later, she was forced to "rephrase" that statement upon cross examination when she couldn't tell my attorney exactly what names I had called her.

Their case further fell apart when we introduced *Miami Herald* reporter Glenn Garvin, who testified that he was

GLENN GARVIN, MIAMI, 2012

JUDGE EDWARD NEWMAN, 2012

on the phone to his editor when
he stumbled upon my arrest and
immediately thought he had walked
into a restricted area and was worried
that he was also going to be arrested.
However, Perez told him not to worry,
that he was in no danger; that they were

"permanently banned" me for taking
pictures of trains.

The truth is, journalism in this country
has always been about activism, starting
with the pamphleteers who encouraged
Americans to revolt against England. It

THE ARAB SPRING

LIBERATION CELEBRATION, LIBYA, 2011

LIBYAN EXPATS, MALTA, 2011

IT ALL STARTED ON DECEMBER 17, 2010 WHEN A 26-YEAR-OLD FRUIT VENDOR NAMED MOHAMED BOUAZIZI SET HIMSELF ON FIRE IN FRONT OF A GOVERNMENT BUILDING IN TUNISIA TO PROTEST AGAINST A POLICEWOMAN WHO HAD CONFISCATED HIS WARES EARLIER THAT DAY.

That led to relatives and other street vendors gathering in front of the same municipal building later that day to protest against the ongoing harassment of the peddlers in this dusty, isolated town of Sidi Bouzid, where unemployment was rampant. That evening, Bouazizi's cousin uploaded a video of the protest to Facebook, the only video-sharing site was not censored by the Tunisian government, where it was picked up by Al Jazeera, a privately owned news network in Qatar that actively scours the Web for citizen journalist videos to broadcast. The video was shaky and grainy but it lit a match in the downtrodden town almost 200 miles outside the nation's capital.

TAHRIR SQUARE, CAIRO, EGYPT, 2011

FREE SYRIAN ARMY (FSA), ALEPPO, SYRIA, 2013

The following day, an even larger crowd consisting of mostly educated but unemployed men demonstrated in front of the building, demanding jobs. As the crowd grew, the demonstration turned violent with men breaking shop windows and police firing tear gas—much of it captured on cell phone video and posted online. "A rock in one hand, a cell phone in the other," Bouazizi's cousin was quoted as saying in *Al Jazeera*.

The state-run media initially ignored, then denied the protests were taking place, then released a statement on December 20, claiming the protests were sparse. But over the next eight days, the world watched videos and photos posted online, showing the protests spreading to other towns as police began shooting real bullets into the crowds, killing at least two men.

On December 27, the protests reached Tunis, the nation's capital, with a thousand people marching in the streets calling for an end to the rampant unemployment. And on December 29, Nessma TV, a privately owned news network, became the first Tunisian news outlet to report on the demonstrations. But by then, the world already knew the country was in the midst of a revolution, having seen the Twitter hash tags go from #bouazizi to #sidibouzid to #tunisia in less than two weeks.

On January 14, ten days after Bouazizi died from his burns, Tunisian President Zine El Abidine Ben Ali fled the country in exile. And in the ensuing months, the protests spread to neighboring Islamic countries, including Algeria, Egypt, Libya and Yemen, which also saw regime changes, as well as to several other countries that did not see regime changes. Had it not been for the internet, the initial protests in Sidi Bouzid would likely have been quashed within days, if even that, and not a word of it would have traveled outside the region. Ben Ali kept a tight reign on information by controlling the state-run media and censoring privately run media since he took over in a 1987 coup d'état.

In 1999, the Committee to Protect Journalists listed him as one of the "10 Worst Enemies of the Press" in a report. Reporters Without Borders called him a leading "Predator of Press Freedom." Most reporters would not dare publish anything critical against Ben Ali, but those who did would end up harassed, intimidated, and jailed. The Tunisian Internet Agency also filtered internet content by controlling the country's sole server, which enabled them to block most foreign sites, especially those critical of his regime, including the two journalist organizations mentioned above, who remained constant critics for more than a decade. They had also

blocked access to YouTube and Facebook, the latter of which Ben Ali reluctantly unblocked a month later in September 2008 after a blogger and a pair of unions filed legal suit against the government. Once accessible, Facebook quickly became a platform for young activists who created pages calling for further internet freedom. On December 7, 2010, ten days before Bouazizi doused himself with paint thinner and set himself on fire, the Tunisian government blocked access to a Lebanese news site that had published U.S. cables from WikiLeaks. *The Guardian* reported:

"The problem is clear," wrote ambassador Robert Godec in July 2009, in a secret dispatch released by Beirut's al-Akhbar newspaper. "Tunisia has been ruled by the same president for 22 years. He has no successor. And, while President Ben Ali deserves credit for continuing many of the progressive policies of President Bourguiba, he and his regime have lost touch with the Tunisian people. They tolerate no advice or criticism, whether domestic or international. Increasingly, they rely

on the police for control and focus on preserving power. Corruption in the inner circle is growing. Even average Tunisians are now keenly aware of it, and the chorus of complaints is rising. Tunisians intensely dislike, even hate, first lady Leïla Trabelsi and her family. In private, regime opponents mock her; even those close to the government express dismay at her reported behaviour. Meanwhile, anger is growing at Tunisia's high unemployment and regional inequities. As a consequence, the risks to the regime's long-term stability are increasing."

So it's not surprising that when Bouazizi doused himself with paint thinner and set himself on fire, the anger over unemployment colluded with the anger over censorship, turning almost every citizen into a journalist. From those on the ground with their cell phones to those at home on their computers, who managed to publish all the content to the Web despite the customary blackout, got it through the governmental media blackout.

DEMONSTRATION WITH MOHAMED BOUAZIZI PICTURED IN BACKGROUND, SOUTH TUNISIA, 2012

DIRTY BLONDES

ON SUNDAY, JUNE 28, 2013, A YOUNG MAN NAMED KEELAN DUMONT WAS IN A PATIO OUTSIDE THE DIRTY BLONDES BAR IN FORT LAUDERDALE, FLORIDA WHEN HE NOTICED AN ARGUMENT BETWEEN TWO MEN AND A GROUP OF BOUNCERS. HE PULLED OUT HIS IPHONE TO BEGIN VIDEO RECORDING, USING HIS INSTAGRAM APP, WHICH HAD JUST INTRODUCED A 15-SECOND VIDEO FEATURE THE PREVIOUS MONTH.

He ended up capturing a violent encounter that ended up going viral, causing widespread outrage among viewers. The shocking video showed a burly bouncer walking behind a patron and placing him in a chokehold before slamming him to the ground followed by a second muscular bouncer punching another patron in the face repeatedly before kicking him in the head after he was already down.

The following day, the *New Times Broward-Palm Beach* posted the video on its website, reporting that Fort Lauderdale police responded to the incident only to arrest the two patrons, Alex Coelho and David Parker, who had been viciously beaten on video, sparking further anger among viewers. From there, I posted the video on my blog along with a write-up and a link to the Dirty Blondes Facebook page and over the next few hours, outraged citizens berated the company on its Facebook page, demanding the bouncers not only be fired, but also arrested on battery charges. Attempting damage control, Dirty Blondes quickly issued a statement on its Facebook page,

FORT LAUDERDALE, FLORIDA, 2013

defending its bouncers, which generated even more hostile comments from citizens. Dirty Blondes ended up removing the statement after more than 100 negative comments and was forced to delete its entire Facebook page, which had about 3,200 likes at the time.

That same night, a Facebook page called Boycott Dirty Blondes emerged and began asking the public for the identities of the security guards, which didn't take long to obtain. After confirming the names with their personal Facebook pages or LinkedIn pages, I posted the photos and names of the bouncers on my blog, something the mainstream media did not do, although they did refer to the Facebook page, informing readers they had the names and photos of the bouncers. The Boycott Dirty Blondes Facebook page became a platform for citizen journalism, with people digging up previous arrest records and mug shots of the bouncers and posting them online, while the mainstream media was still refusing to identify them. And then came the Yelp reviews where hundreds of negative comments took it from a 4.5 rating to a rating of one, which is the lowest any business can go.

The next day, the video ended up going even more viral when *The Huffington Post* ran it as well as all the local news stations and newspapers. After a week of social media outrage, Fort Lauderdale police announced that two of the bouncers, Arnald Thomas-Darrah and Jovan Ralfhel Dean, would be criminally charged. And charges were dropped against Coelho and Parker a few weeks later.

Keelan Dumont never set out to be a citizen journalist when he recorded the video of the altercation and uploaded it to Instagram. In fact, he ended up removing the video, then setting his Instagram account to private after all the attention it started receiving. And he never responded to my request for interviews. I had a feeling he would remove the video, so I had downloaded it from his account and reposted it to my YouTube account, which was technically a copyright violation (see pages 118–119), but I did it

in the name of public interest. He apparently had sent the video to the local media before removing it because they all started airing the video in their news segments. From there, it was uploaded multiple times to YouTube and LiveLeak, so there was no stopping its virality (do a search for "Dirty Blondes Bouncers" to check it out). And from there, the story was reported in news sites throughout the world.

Meanwhile, the Boycott Dirty Blondes Facebook page racked up more than 8,000 likes in less than a week, more than double of what the original Dirty Blondes Facebook page had before it was deactivated. That page quickly became a platform for citizens who within 24 hours of the page going live, posted the names, photos and even past criminal records of the bouncers. And that was followed by several people reporting their own violent encounters with the bouncers, followed by another YouTube video from 2010 showing a Dirty Blondes bouncer knocking out a man during a brawl in front of the bar.

By the following day, Fort Lauderdale police issued a press release stating the following:

"The Fort Lauderdale Police Department is aware of the short clip that has been circulating via YouTube and social media, and we are looking into the details surrounding this incident. At this time, there have been no reports filed with this agency depicting the incident that was captured on this video. The agency encourages both of the individuals arrested to come forward and file police reports regarding the altercation that took place prior to officers' arrival."

The truth is, both men were arrested after returning to the bar, bloodied and beat-up, and understandably angry. Police accused them of trying to pick a fight with the bouncers while the men claimed they were trying to inform police of what had taken place. However, because Fort Lauderdale police frequently worked off-duty at the bar (a common practice for police officers in South Florida, where they get paid by a private establishment to work security detail), they had a natural inclination to take the bouncers' word as to what led to the altercation.

They arrested the men without question, not bothering to get witness statements, even though both men were visibly injured. And they would have left it at that had it not been for the 15-second Instagram video, followed by the Boycott Dirty Blondes Facebook page, which proved to be a community collaboration of citizen journalism that not only sought justice, but achieved it.

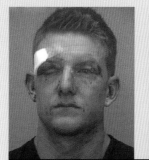

THE TWO VICTIMS (*LEFT, CENTER*), AND BOUNCER ARNALD THOMAS-DARRAH (*RIGHT*)

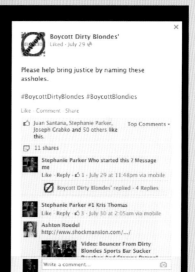

Boycott Dirty Blondes'
Liked · July 29

Please help bring justice by naming these assholes.

#BoycottDirtyBlondes #BoycottBlondies

Like · Comment · Share

Juan Santana, Stephanie Parker, Joseph Grabko and 50 others like this.   Top Comments ▾

11 shares

Stephanie Parker Who started this ? Message me
Like · Reply · 👍 1 · July 29 at 11:48pm via mobile

Boycott Dirty Blondes' replied · 4 Replies

Stephanie Parker #1 Kris Thomas
Like · Reply · 👍 3 · July 30 at 2:05am via mobile

Ashton Roedel
http://www.shockmansion.com/.../

Video: Bouncer From Dirty Blondes Sports Bar Sucker

Write a comment...

THE COP WATCHERS

COPWATCH.com
POLICING THE POLICE

A YEAR BEFORE A GROUP OF LOS ANGELES POLICE OFFICERS WERE CAUGHT ON CAMERA BEATING A MAN DURING A TRAFFIC STOP IN A VIDEO CONSIDERED TO BE A MILESTONE FOR CITIZEN JOURNALISM, A GROUP OF ACTIVISTS IN NORTHERN CALIFORNIA WERE ALREADY ON THE STREETS VIDEOTAPING POLICE.

Copwatch launched in Berkeley in March 1990, exactly a year before the Rodney King beating video shocked the world, because police were preying on homeless people and minorities in an area that was being gentrified. By the end of the decade, Copwatch had chapters throughout the United States. But while Copwatch did an excellent job on educating citizens about their rights through DVDs and seminars, the organization did not capitalize on the launching of YouTube in 2005, mainly because it never got into the habit of making the videos public, using them mostly as trial evidence in instances where citizens were wrongly arrested.

However, a new generation of cop watchers emerged through YouTube, many whose videos found a home on my blog after I launched it in 2007, which I'm proud to say, was the first site dedicated to documenting instances of police arresting citizens with cameras regardless of whether they were professional journalists, street photographers or citizens merely using their phone to record their interaction with police.

FTAA PROTESTS, MIAMI, 2003

In May 2009, I wrote about a group of libertarian activists who were arrested for video recording cops during a traffic stop in Mississippi as they were traveling the country in a recreational vehicle. That incident prompted the activists, Adam "Ademo Freeman" Mueller, Pete Eyre and Jason Talley, to launch a site called *Cop Block* in January 2010. Based in New Hampshire, *Cop Block* encouraged activists throughout the country to launch their own chapter of *Cop Block* where today, they have chapters in almost all fifty states.

In January 2012, I wrote about a West Point graduate named Antonio Buehler, who was arrested after photographing police manhandling a woman during a DWI stop at an Austin gas station. After Buehler snapped his photo, one of the officers stormed up to him and shoved him against his car, arresting him on charges of felony assault on a police officer, claiming that Buehler had spit in his face, a charge that carries a prison sentence of ten years. What the cops didn't realize was that another citizen had been video recording the encounter from across the street, showing no

evidence that Buehler had spit on Austin police officer Pat Oborski.

But when prosecutors refused to drop the charges against Buehler, he and a few other activists launched the Peaceful Streets Project where activists would roam the streets of Austin, video recording police as they interacted with the public in an effort to hold them accountable.

Today, Peaceful Streets has chapters in several states and is growing fast. And Buehler was eventually acquitted.

Throughout the 20th century, police in the United States were able to maintain a polished, professional image in the eyes of most Americans. Sure, there have always been complaints about police brutality within black neighborhoods—one of the reasons that led to Copwatch—but most Americans were led to believe those claims were either exaggerated or a result of officers defending themselves from violent criminals, as they normally claimed. On those occasions that videos did surface showing police brutality, police were able to convince the public that they were just isolated incidents from a few bad apples.

However, that all began to change with the inception of YouTube, which hosted an endless stream of citizen videos showing police abusing their powers, many times not realizing they were being recorded, but many times also knowing full well they were being recorded as they threatened, intimidated and arrested citizens for recording them in public. But there is no law against recording cops in public, no matter how hard police tried to make people believe. In fact, the more they abused their power on camera, the more these videos would spread throughout the internet, revealing a much darker side to the police force than most people had seen before, prompting even more people to start recording cops, resulting in even more unlawful arrests. It became clear that

COPWATCH ACTION, CALIFORNIA, 2005

APR 13 2005
9:34:40 PM

police, for years, had become accustomed to creating their own truths in their arrest reports, which were never questioned before the judges and juries. Until the emergence of YouTube, that is, which is why they feared cameras more than guns.

It got to the point where the United States Department of Justice had to issue a set of guidelines for police departments to follow when dealing with citizens recording them, citing numerous examples of case law confirming that citizens not only had the right to record cops, but that police had almost no authority to confiscate cameras. However, police never fail to come up with new ways to arrest citizens, including using outdated wiretapping laws or making ludicrous statements that they were in fear for their lives because they perceived the camera to be a gun.

So even though the law is on our side, it doesn't mean police will refrain from arresting us, which is why it makes sense to record cops in larger groups where everybody is carrying a camera rather than going out alone where you are extremely vulnerable. But you just never know when you might come across a police interaction that deserves to be recorded when you are alone, which is why it makes sense to use live-streaming apps on your phones such as Bambuser, Qik and Ustream just in case they do arrest you and confiscate your phone. It also makes sense to keep your phone locked with a password to prevent cops from attempting to delete your video.

More importantly, it makes sense to not break any other laws as you are recording police by interfering, standing on a street or on private property after being asked to leave. And it can't be stressed hard enough, please hold your phone in the horizontal position to avoid the annoying vertical video syndrome. For more advice on recording cops, Google "Ten Rules for Recording Cops (and Other Authority Figures)," which can be found on my blog.

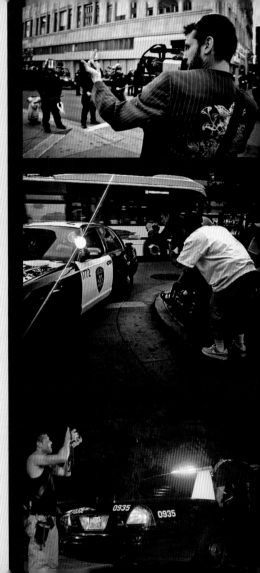

KELLY THOMAS

THE FIRST YOUTUBE VIDEO THAT EMERGED FROM THE KELLY THOMAS TRAGIC DEATH DID NOT EVEN SHOW THE BEATING. BUT IT CAPTURED THOMAS' HORRIFIC SCREAMS. AND THE JOLTING SOUNDS OF A POLICE TASER. AND THE ANGUISHED PLEAS FOR HIS FATHER, WHICH PIERCED THE OTHERWISE PEACEFUL CALIFORNIAN NIGHT.

"Dad! ... Dad! ... Dad!" the 37-year-old mentally ill homeless man yelled as six Fullerton police officers beat, kicked, tased, and suffocated him at a city bus depot on July 5, 2011.

But it was the video that was released almost a year after his death from the city's surveillance camera, which also included audio from the officers' body-mounted recorders, that shocked the world.

"See these fists," Fullerton police officer Manny Ramos can be heard saying after donning a pair of latex gloves as he stood over Thomas, who is sitting on the curb passively. "These fists are about to fuck you up."

Within seconds, Ramos and his partner, Joe Wolfe, were beating Thomas with their batons.

"I'm sorry! I'm sorry!" Thomas yelled as they pounced on him, apologizing for whatever it was he had done to tick them off.

With their full body weight on him, both cops kept ordering him to "place your hands behind your back"—even though one of his arms was lodged beneath his body. One cop can be seen kicking him repeatedly as Thomas yelled, "I can't breathe!" Two more cops arrive, one who starts tasering him, sending Thomas' body into convulsions, causing him to shriek in pain, ordering him to roll onto his stomach and tasering him repeatedly when he didn't immediately comply. And two more cops came speeding up in their patrol cars, prompting one of the four cops on top

of Thomas to momentarily pause from beating him with a flashlight and look up to say, "help us." But the only one who needed help was Thomas, who kept yelling, "help me, dad, help me, dad" as the cops kept telling him to "stop resisting."

Even as his pleas for help became weaker and his gasps for life became shorter and his clumped body became visible to the camera for the first time in almost ten minutes of the officers being

piled on top of him, punching him, kicking him, tasing him and beating him with a flashlight and taser gun, one cop examining him can be heard saying:

"He's still fighting."

But he was not fighting and had never been fighting.

The truth is, the 165-pound man who suffered from schizophrenia was known within the Fullerton community as a

KELLY THOMAS MURDER TRIAL, CALIFORNIA, 2012

gentle soul who would pick up cigarette butts from the parking lots around the bus depot as he had been doing that night before he was confronted by cops.

Although about 50 people had witnessed the beating, including at least one person who video recorded it but had his camera confiscated, Fullerton police went into instant damage control mode, claiming that Thomas had been breaking into cars, then started fighting with the officers when they tried to arrest him. They also claimed he had fought them so hard, that two of the six cops were left with broken bones, information that was run by the media without questioning. But that all turned out to be lies. Nevertheless, the media lost interest in the story after Thomas died five days after the beating, writing it off as nothing but a "scuffle" between six officers and a homeless man.

Meanwhile, Thomas' father, Ron Thomas, a retired Orange County sheriff's deputy who had been seeking witnesses, was embarking on a personal crusade to seek justice for his son. And a local blog named *Friends of Fullerton's Future* was also embarking on a crusade to expose the truth, questioning the police version of the story from the onset, being the first to point out that the beating was most likely captured on the city's surveillance video, as well as interviewing witnesses on camera. So when the media refused to run a photo Ron Thomas had taken of his son's grotesquely swollen face in the hospital, he turned to the blog, which was operated by a man named Tony Bushala along with several other bloggers who normally covered local politics.

The blog not only was the first website to publish the horrific photo, they were also the first to post the video recorded by a bystander that captured Thomas' chilling screams. And from there, the story went international with the *Daily Mail* in the United Kingdom picking up the story along with several national news sites. And in the ensuing months, *Friends of Fullerton's Future* consistently remained ahead of the pack on the story, being the first to reveal the names of the officers involved in the beating, which they obtained from internal sources. It then successfully led a recall effort against three city councilmen who had stoutly defended the cops involved in the beating. The Orange County District Attorney eventually filed murder and manslaughter charges against some of the officers involved. They were acquitted of all charges in January 2014.

The Kelly Thomas case revealed the uneasy relationship police have established with the media where police are not only able to control the facts, but able to manipulate the truth to justify any shooting or beating in the name of officer safety. And most of the time, the media accepts the conditions of this relationship in order not to lose access to information steadily provided by police.

Even though Ron Thomas was persistent in his efforts to spread the truth about his son, he would never have been able to do so without the help of *Friends of Fullerton's Future*.

OCCUPY WALL STREET

OWS PROTEST, NEW YORK CITY, 2011

FOR MORE THAN A WEEK THE MAINSTREAM MEDIA EITHER IGNORED, RIDICULED OR DOWNPLAYED THE EXISTENCE OF THE PROTESTERS THAT HAD SWARMED LOWER MANHATTAN, SETTING UP CAMP IN ZUCCOTTI PARK ON SEPTEMBER 17, 2011. THAT IS, UNTIL A COP NICKNAMED "TONY BALONEY" PEPPER SPRAYED A GROUP OF ACTIVISTS WHO WERE ALREADY CORRALLED BY POLICE IN ORANGE NETTING, AND SHOWING NO SIGNS OF AGGRESSION OR RESISTANCE.

The officer's real name was Anthony Bologna and he was a commander with the New York City Police Department, a 29-year veteran who should have known better. But the phenomenon of almost every citizen carrying a camera during protests was rather new, inspired by the Arab Spring uprising from earlier that year. So Bologna figured he would get away with reaching over another police officer and pepper spraying the activists before slipping back into the crowd on

If the Occupy Wall Street protesters ever choose to recognize a person who gave their cause its biggest boost, they may want to pay tribute to Anthony Bologna. Deputy Inspector Bologna, to be more precise, was the senior New York police officer who on Sept. 24 blasted pepper spray at four female demonstrators, knocking them to the sidewalk in pain. An oft-viewed video of that moment offers no evidence of their having posed a threat or doing anything more sinister than shouting.

September 24, leaving several activists rubbing their eyes, including two women temporarily blinded with burning eyes as they screeched in pain. However, it was all caught on video and uploaded to Youtube two days later by the hacker activist group Anonymous.

As the video went viral, the media began reporting on it, quoting an NYPD spokesman accusing the activists of selective editing, insisting that Bologna acted "appropriately." But then a second video emerged showing Bologna pepper spraying another group of activists, which is when the media started becoming a little more sympathetic to the protesters. And it was also when Occupy encampments began springing up in other cities throughout the country, including Los Angeles, San Francisco and Boston, and eventually throughout the world. By then, it really didn't matter what the mainstream media was reporting. People were forming their own opinions on the movement through an endless stream of Youtube videos posted by activists. According to an October 11, 2011 article in *The New York Times*:

That pepper shot in the face was a vital shot in the arm for the nascent anti-Wall Street movement.

Its takeover of Zuccotti Park in Lower Manhattan had begun a week earlier, drawing some attention but not a lot—for a reason. Despite the belief of many protesters in their own uniqueness, this is a city inured to countless demonstrations held over a good many decades.

Inspector Bologna's improvidence was a game change.

Up until the Bologna videos, the mainstream media had taken the typical institutionalized approach when covering Occupy Wall Street, mostly quoting politicians and police as the official version of the story while treating the activists as fringes of society, criticizing them for having no clear message and mocking them for their idealism. But Occupy Wall Street's message was obvious to anybody paying attention, not to mention that it was, and still is, stated on www.occupywallst.org, the site they launched months earlier in order to document the occupation. The country had been in an economic downturn since President George W. Bush and it wasn't getting better in the third year of Barack Obama's presidency. Despite Obama's promise of change, the wealth in this country was becoming increasingly more concentrated in the hands of a fewer corporations.

However, the mainstream media, which had gone through its own share of downsizing and conglomeration, still acted blind as to what the protesters were griping about. Remember, in 1980, 50 companies controlled 90% of the American media when by 2013, six companies controlled the same. Which is why the activists never expected any real coverage. Instead, they planned to document and publish their own news as it happened by livestreaming everything, from the moment they took over, to their website. They also posted photos and videos to Flickr, Facebook, Twitter, Youtube, and LiveLeak.

Three days after the first Bologna video was posted, Occupy Wall Street raised $12,000 in eight hours to launch the movement's own newspaper, the *Occupy Wall Street Journal*, with an initial print run of 50,000 copies that were handed out to people in Lower

OWS PROTEST, NEW YORK CITY, 2011

Manhattan's financial district. On October 1, tensions between the NYPD and the activists escalated with the arrest of 700 protesters on the Brooklyn Bridge. The activists claimed that cops purposely led them onto the bridge in order to arrest them. And they had dozens of videos to back up their claims. Police responded with their own Youtube video, showing them warning protesters not to go on the bridge or else face arrest. Amazingly—but not surprisingly—only one credentialed journalist was within the corralled crowd when they were all arrested, a freelancer for *The New York Times* named Natasha Lennard, who ended up having to cut ties with the newspaper after she openly admitted her support for the movement.

The multitude of videos popping up online from the Brooklyn Bridge mass arrest further inspired several other Occupy encampments throughout the United States, including Occupy Los Angeles, Occupy Boston and Occupy San Francisco, and later, Occupy Miami, Occupy Atlanta and many more.

It was around this time that notable livestreamers Timothy Pool (@Timcast) covering Occupy Wall Street and Spencer Mills (@OakFoSho) covering Occupy Oakland added a new dimension to journalism by allowing viewers to either direct them or ask them questions through live chat as they were livestreaming. It got to the point where the mainstream media had become completely irrelevant to the movement, even though they finally started covering it.

THE OSCAR GRANT SHOOTING

IT WAS JUST TWO HOURS INTO 2009 AND THE BAY AREA RAPID TRANSIT SYSTEM WAS FILLED WITH FESTIVE AND ROWDY COMMUTERS TRAVELING TO OAKLAND AFTER HAVING CELEBRATED NEW YEAR'S EVE IN SAN FRANCISCO. TWO GROUPS OF MEN WERE ENGAGED IN A CONFRONTATION INSIDE A TRAIN CAR. THERE WAS SOME PUSHING AND SHOVING AND MAYBE A COUPLE OF THROWN PUNCHES. WITNESSES CALLED 911. BART POLICE WERE DISPATCHED AS THE TRAIN CAME TO A COMPLETE STOP AT THE FRUITVALE STATION IN OAKLAND.

Officer Tony Pirone had his taser out when he confronted a group of black men wearing black clothes, which matched the description of the radio call. Pirone was very aggressive and profane, according to several witness testimonies, who all said he escalated a situation that had already ended. A few people pulled out their phones and started recording. The videos show Pirone punching a man named Oscar Grant, then forcing him down to a sitting position as a crowd of boisterous commuters protested. More BART cops came running up, including a rookie named Johannes Mehserle. The people got louder, chanting, "let them go!" And they got even louder as Pirone and Mehserle started dragging Grant face down on the platform in order to handcuff him. Pirone placed his knee on Grant's head as Mehserle tried to place Grant's hands behind his back. Mehserle then stood over Grant and pulled out his gun, firing a single shot into the young man's back.

The loud bang silenced the crowd for a second as they came to the shocked realization they had just witnessed a cop shooting a man in the back. A non-resistant man with no visible weapons.

"They just shot him!" several people can be heard exclaiming in disbelief. "They just shot him!"

In the ensuing moments, BART police began seizing cell phone cameras from witnesses but several managed to leave the scene with their phones as the train shut its doors and departed the station. Later that day, the story of the shooting was reported in the local media with sparse details and sparking absolutely

OAKLAND, 2009

no interest outside the Oakland area. But on January 3, 2009, Oakland television station KTVU aired a segment that included two cell phone videos they had obtained from witnesses, but only after warning viewers the videos could be disturbing, uploading the segment to YouTube the following day where it started going viral. More videos emerged in the following days, including one with an even a clearer view of the shooting than the first two, and people in the community began protesting. On January 13, after heavy pressure from the locals as well as thousands on the internet, the Alameda County District Attorney filed murder charges against Mehserle. He was convicted of manslaughter more than a year later, serving 11 months in jail before being released.

Johannes Mehserle would not have spent a day in jail had it not been for the multiple witnesses with cameras that recorded him shooting an unarmed man in the back. In fact, he became the first

OSCAR GRANT MURDER TRIAL PROTESTS, OAKLAND, 2009

cop in California history to be charged with murder over an incident taking place while on duty. However, things might have turned out differently had BART officers succeeded in confiscating everybody's cameras as they tried to do. Five citizen videos were introduced as evidence during the June 2010 trial as well as a sixth video from the train station's surveillance video, something BART officials initially said had not been working on the night of the shooting.

Of those five, three were posted on the internet within days of the shooting. The other two were from phones police had confiscated and introduced during the trial. To get a solid grasp of the entire incident, find a YouTube video titled "Captured by 6 different cameras BART police shoot and kill unarmed Oscar Grant," and watch it on a full screen. The first citizen to turn on a camera was Karina Vargas, who was then a 19-year-old receptionist. This is how she explained the moments after Grant was shot it in an article she wrote for Redwood Cop Watch on February 20, 2009:

That's when a lady officer approaches me and she's telling me: "Give me that camera! Give me that camera!" And in the video, you see the BART doors close on her face. She's banging on the door, like "Give me that camera!" You can hear her in the video, I'm like: "F--- no! You're not getting this camera!" Because I knew why else does she want the camera? I got something good and I knew what I had. I was like uh-uh, this is not right. I'm going to show this to the world, because this is not okay. They didn't want the fact that they knew they had shot someone in the back, who was already willingly laying on his belly, with his arms behind his back, not fidgeting, not fighting, not being defiant whatsoever. That's why they tried to get the camera.

In the ensuing days, more videos emerged, including one that provided the clearest view as well as the best audio. The Oscar Grant shooting was a milestone for citizen journalism in that so many people with absolutely no journalistic background had the instincts to pull out their phones to start recording. Even Oscar Grant had this

instinct as he was sitting against the wall, moments before he was killed, and used his phone to photograph Mehserle pointing a taser gun at him in a photo he sent to his girlfriend, who was waiting below, telling her, "They're beating us up for no reason, I'll call you back."

THE FUTURE

MEETUP WITH RADLEY BALKO, AUSTIN, TEXAS, 2013

A FEW YEARS AGO, THE QUESTION WAS WHETHER CITIZEN JOURNALISM WAS CREDIBLE ENOUGH TO GET THE FACTS STRAIGHT, NOT TO MENTION SUSTAINABLE ENOUGH TO REGULARLY PRODUCE CONTENT. NOW THE QUESTION SEEMS TO BE WHETHER THE CORPORATE MEDIA IS CREDIBLE ENOUGH TO DELIVER FACTS WITHOUT AN INSTITUTIONALIZED FILTER, NOT TO MENTION SUSTAINABLE ENOUGH TO SURVIVE CONSTANT DOWNSIZING, LAYOFFS AND MERGERS.

In fact, the biggest news story of 2013 was broken by a citizen journalist named Glenn Greenwald, who through documents leaked by whistleblower Edward Snowden, exposed a vast surveillance program conducted by the National Security Agency, which pried into the lives of thousands of Americans who had not committed crimes. On the day his report was published, the *Chicago Sun-Times*, which had the ninth-highest circulation in the country and eight Pulitzer Prizes under its belt, was laying off its entire photo staff, ordering reporters with no professional photography experience to begin taking photos with their iPhones. So clearly, quality journalism is no longer restricted to the so-called professionals.

However, Greenwald, a former attorney turned blogger turned investigative reporter, who calls himself an activist and advocate—labels a mainstream media journalist would never use—published his reports in *The Guardian* and *The Washington Post*, two mainstream media newspapers that gave Greenwald's story exposure on both sides of the Atlantic. But even then, Greenwald remained a frequent critic of the mainstream media's insistence on remaining objective, criticizing it as simply hiding one's biases. And by the end of 2013, he had quit his gig at *The Guardian* to join a new journalistic venture financed by eBay founder Pierre Omidyar; only weeks after Amazon founder Jeff Bezos purchased *The Washington Post*, signifying a shift from the corporate media conglomerates towards the technology sector.

Radley Balko, an opinion blogger for *The Washington Post*—whose highly successful blog, *The Agitator*, inspired me to keep pounding away at my blog during the early years, knowing there was an audience out there for opinionated (but transparent) journalism—believes most daily newspapers will eventually die off, leaving only the ones with a national scope in print. He also believes citizen journalism will continue to rise with more people turning to the internet to share stories of social injustice, government abuse and police accountability. And he believes more non-profit or philanthropy-funded news sites dedicated to investigative journalism will emerge, providing an outlet for both professional and citizen journalists. But the death of newspapers will still leave a void.

"The death of the daily newspaper is going to leave some gaping holes in coverage of more mundane, less sexy beats like city council meetings, state and local government budgets, local education, and so on," he said.

"Newspapers have provided an important archive of public records in these areas, so I'd love to see active, involved citizens and community journalism projects pick up the slack."

Hopefully, this book will help you get started.

POLITICAL RALLY, PARIS, FRANCE, 2012

INDEX

INDEX & PICTURE CREDITS

ACKNOWLEDGMENTS

First and foremost, I would like to thank Miami Police Sergeant Ronald Rahming and officers Anthonius Kurver, Maykel Baluja, and Marvalyn Reid for arresting me in 2007 after I photographed them making an arrest, one of whom repeatedly bashed my head into the sidewalk after they tackled, then piled on top of me, twisting my arms behind my back and ordering me to "stop resisting" when I was just trying to protect my cameras. Although the knot on my forehead, the pain in my wrists, and the bruises, scrapes, and aches throughout my body eventually subsided, the fire in my heart raged on, driving me to launch my blog and turn it into a national clearing house for these types of incidents, an issue I discovered was epidemic.

Let me also thank Miami Beach police officer David Socarras, who arrested me in 2009 after I photographed him leaning against a car during the controversial hip hop weekend. I was one of almost 600 arrested that Memorial Day Weekend, the only one who recovered the photos they deleted, then plastered the officer's name and photo all over the internet in the weeks leading to my trial, which is why he never showed up, even though they gave him three chances.

And let me not forget Miami-Dade Major Nancy Perez—a media spokesperson who should have known better, but who arrested me during the Occupy Miami eviction in 2012. Although she also had my footage deleted, I recovered that as well, drawing attention from prominent national news sites that may have otherwise ignored the arrest as one of hundreds that were taking place during the Occupy protests. She did show up to trial, but proved unable to spin the facts as she has done so many times in her career as a spokesperson.

In trying to suppress my right to free speech, you officers built me a humongous platform that became a thorn in the side for hundreds of other police officers throughout the country.

All those cops on my blog? The ones embarrassing themselves in videos that go viral ten times over?

They owe it all to you.

And finally, a very sincere thank you to my mom, who more than once waited for me outside the jail even though I told her not to, then sat through my trials, not to mention read every single word I wrote on my blog since the beginning.

I owe it all to you.